True Secrets of Salt Lake City and The Great Salt Lake Revealed!

Cover design by: Greg Needham | Greg Needham Design & Graphics

FIRST EDITION

Inquiries should be addressed to:

Eden Entertainment Limited, Inc.
1107 Key Plaza #195
Key West, Florida 33040

www.TrueSecretsOf.com

LIBRARY OF CONGRESS
CATALOGING IN PUBLICATION DATA

Eden Entertainment Limited, Inc.
True Secrets of Salt Lake City and The Great Salt Lake Revealed!
First Edition

Printed in the United States of America

Coming soon...

True Secrets of Alaska Revealed!
July 2002

True Secrets of New Orleans Revealed!
January 2003

True Secrets of Washington D.C. Revealed!
March 2003

to a book store near you!

About the Authors

Scott Gutelius has had a long and distinguished career of jaywalking, a tradition he continued while doing research in and around Salt Lake City. By the end of his time there, he estimates to have jaywalked well over 200 times, completely shunning crosswalks (when there were crosswalks to be shunned) and even jumping a few fast-moving bumpers. Much to his chagrin, he was never ticketed. Last we heard, he was still nursing his bumpercar wounds on the beach near his filthy apartment in Key West.

Scott Gutelius

Marshall Stone has moved quietly through life in the grip of three manias. He has a fascination with historical architecture, utter devotion to classical music and its performance (as pipe organ designer, teacher, pianist, organist and harpsichordist), and is in wonder at the world of model railroading. Unfortunately, the trains are still in the box waiting at the station. As of late, the mellifluous colours of the English language have drawn him to this present project, editing the hackneyed work of Eden Entertainment writers.

Marshall Stone

Marcus Varner spent many of his formative years attempting to graduate from Weber High School in North Ogden Utah. He was finally successful and went on to an illustrious career picking cherries and working at a local amusement park. His penchant for collecting obscure minutiae led him to assist the authors of this book and help organize their thoughts on historical trivia. Marcus has never floated in the Great Salt Lake but he did once race his mini van on the Bonneville Salt Flats.

Marcus Varner

Daniel Reynen has been a tinman, salesman, laborer and grunt. In the last year he has immersed himself in the history of Utah to the exclusion of almost everything else. While visiting the Kennecott Bingham Canyon Mine he listened patiently as the tour guide explained the various metals they were excavating. As he surveyed the vast open pit he turned to the guide and asked, "did they find what they were looking for?" His innocence has been a welcome refuge for the normally skeptical writers.

Daniel Reynen

Contents

Early Utah

Who were the first inhabitants of Salt Lake?

The earliest known are called Paleo-Indians by archeologists. They were hunter-gatherers and can be traced back more than 10,000 years. Changes began to appear 8,000 years ago in a time known as the archaic period. Paleo-indians were still hunter gatherers and nomadic but also lived in semi-permanent small villages and caves.

(OK, it's sounding like a James A. Michener novel, can we move things along?)

Around 2,500 years ago the next big changes began when corn, beans and squash were introduced into Utah. The peoples that occupied Utah at that time were known as the Fremont and Anasazi; both disappeared from the archeological record around AD 1300.

Were there people in Utah when the Mormon settlers arrived in 1847?

Yes, the Goshute, Navajo, Northern Shoshone, Eastern Shoshone, Southern Paiute and Ute. All of them but the Navajo speak different but related languages from a family known as the Numic language family. The Navajo speak a language that is from the Athabascan language family.

The Ute lived throughout much of Utah and in historic times at least eleven different bands of the Ute Tribe were identified. The state of Utah is named after the Ute.

Who was the first non-Indian to enter the state of Utah?

Juan Maria Rivera. He led at least two expeditions in 1765 into what would become Utah. In July of 1776 a ten man exploration team headed by two Franciscan priests, Dominguez and Escalante, traversed the Uinta Basin, crossed the Wasatch Mountains and visited the Indian encampment at Utah Lake.

The diary kept by Father Escalante, the Rivera journals and a map made by Bernardo de Miera, who accompanied the Dominguez Escalante party, are the first written documents in Utah's history.

Explorers and traders continued to be interested in Utah and by the early 1800s trade between Santa Fe and the Indians in north-central Utah had become fairly well established.

Painting of Father Escalante and Father Dominguez in the Utah State Capitol building.

Who explored Utah next?

Mostly mountain men such as Jedediah Smith, William Sublette and James Clyman. They explored, hunted and trapped throughout Utah, Oregon and California, providing valuable information for future immigrations.

It was the mountain men who would develop South Pass, the regular route through the Rocky Mountains. Another mountain man named Jim Bridger was reported to have discovered the Great Salt Lake in 1824 when he made a bet with other trappers about the course of the Bear River. He supposedly floated down the river in a boat made out of buffalo skins and entered the Great Salt Lake.

Why did Mormon settlers move to Utah?

Because of persecution and an assassination. In June of 1844 the founder of The Church of Jesus Christ of Latter-day Saints, Joseph Smith, Jr., and his brother Hyrum were assassinated in the town of Carthage, Illinois. A brilliant and energetic man named Brigham Young along with other Church of Jesus Christ leaders decided to abandon the town of Nauvoo, Illinois and move west. They began their trek on February 4, 1846.

The "Mormon migration" was markedly different from migrations before it for several reasons. It was for religious rather than economic causes and the immigrants were primarily women and children. Previous migrations were mainly men in search of conquest for exploration or economic gain. Brigham Young would later be called "The American Moses" for his leadership of this group of settlers.

The first Mormon settlers were a small band of 143 men, three women, two children, 70 wagons, one boat, one cannon, 93 horses, 52 mules, 66 oxen and 19 cows. They arrived in the Salt Lake Valley on July 24, 1847.

Carte-de-visite of Brigham Young, circa 1876, by C.W. Carter. Courtesy Ken Sanders Rare Books, Salt Lake City.

I heard somewhere that Brigham Young was considered the best-educated man of his day. How much time did he spend in school?

A whopping eleven days of formal schooling, and that was by a traveling schoolmaster. How times have changed! After all, to be a leader today requires at least a "C" average in school.

Brigham Young was born in a log cabin in 1801 at Whitingham, Vermont. At fourteen he hired out as an apprentice to learn the trades of carpenter, cabinetmaker, painter and glazier. His mother taught him to read. From these beginnings he would lead the Mormon settlers to Salt Lake City, lay the groundwork for agricultural and industrial development, serve as territorial governor and bring thousands of colonists from all parts of the world to settle in the West.

He also managed to marry twenty six wives and father fifty six children by sixteen of those wives.

Didn't Brigham Young also design a "new and improved" alphabet?

He tried. Young was convinced that there should be an easier way to read and write English for new Church of Jesus Christ converts from other countries. This had nothing to do with his eleven days of schooling. He proceeded to spend thousands of dollars developing the Deseret Alphabet.

Did Brigham Young actually develop the Alphabet himself?

No, he enlisted the help of George D. Watt, an Englishman who had converted to The Church of Jesus Christ in 1837. Watt used a phonetic alphabet known as Pitman Shorthand for a model when he developed the Deseret Alphabet.

What made the Deseret Alphabet so much better than the one we use today?

Every letter had only one sound, eliminating the ambiguity over how a word should be spelled or pronounced. For example there was one letter for the long *a* sound in ate and another letter for the *ah* sound in art. The Deseret Alphabet had 38 characters.

Did anybody use the Deseret Alphabet?

Some started to. The Board of Regents of the University of Deseret and the government of the Territory of Utah both officially adopted it in January of 1854. There were four books printed using the Alphabet, including *The Deseret First Book*, *The Deseret Second Book*, *The Book of Nephi* (not to be confused with the drink Nehi) and *The Book of Mormon*. The *Deseret News* (a Church of Jesus Christ-owned newspaper) on occasion published passages of scripture using the Alphabet. The Deseret Alphabet even appeared on some Mormon money and a tombstone in Cedar City, Utah.

What was the ultimate fate of the Deseret Alphabet?

The advantages of the Deseret phonetic Alphabet were outweighed by its disadvantages; such as the time it would take to teach the symbols to thousands of pioneers and the enormous cost to translate and reprint books. When Brigham Young died in 1877 the Alphabet died with him.

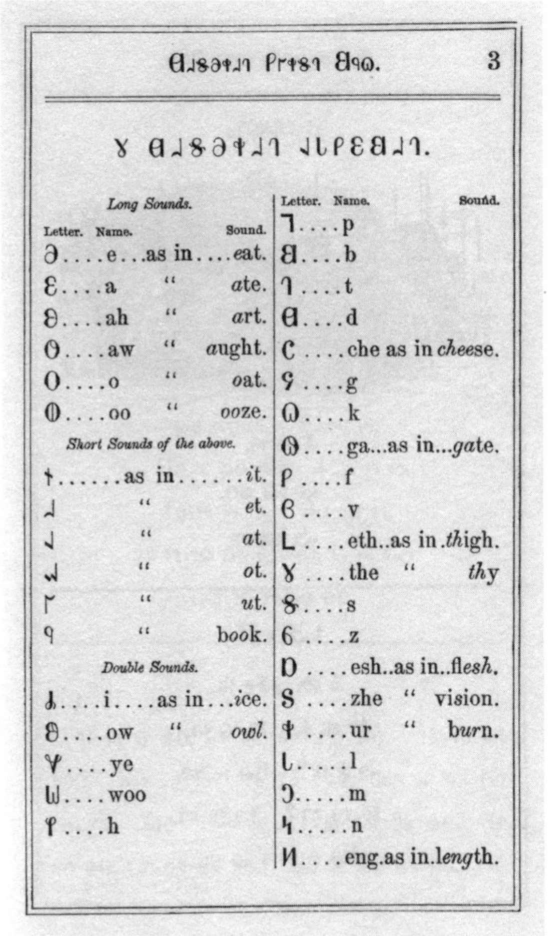

Long Sounds.			Letter.	Name.	Sound.
Letter.	Name.	Sound.	ꓶ	.... p	
Ꝺ	.... e ...as in .... eat.		ꓭ	.... b	
�	.... a " ate.		ꓡ	.... t	
ꝺ	.... ah " art.		ꓷ	.... d	
ꝋ	.... aw " aught.		C	.... che as in *cheese*.	
O	.... o " oat.		ꝯ	.... g	
ꝺ	.... oo " ooze.		ꝋ	.... k	
Short Sounds of the above.			ꝼ	.... ga...as in...*gate*.	
†	...... as in ...... it.		P	.... f	
ꓩ	" et.		ꓭ	 v	
ꓩ	" at.		L	.... eth..as in *thigh*.	
ꓪ	" ot.		ꓵ	.... the " *thy*	
ꓩ	" ut.		ꝸ	.... s	
ꝯ	" book.		6	.... z	
Double Sounds.			D	.... esh..as in *flesh*.	
ꓩ	.... i .... as in ...*ice*.		S	.... zhe " vision.	
ꓭ	.... ow " owl.		ꝸ	.... ur " burn.	
Ꝡ	.... ye		ꓶ	 l	
Ꝡ	.... woo		ꓳ	..... m	
ꝼ	.... h		ꓩ	..... n	
			Ꝺ	.... eng.as in.*length*.	

A sample of the Deseret Alphabet. Photo used by permission, Deseret Village ZCMI Store in This is The Place Park.

When did the Mormons settle Salt Lake City?

An advance party of Mormons entered Salt Lake Valley July 22, 1847. Within two days, planting, irrigation and exploration of the surrounding area began.

What did Brigham Young say in a letter to one of his sons in college?

"P.S. Be sure and don't study so hard as to injure your health."

Did former President George Bush Sr. say the same thing to his older son?

Not to our knowledge.

What did the early pioneers use for money?

The barter system was used quite extensively but The Church of Jesus Christ also issued currency. Gold dust was used in many places but was hard to handle. So, in 1848 handwritten "valley notes" were issued in denominations of 50¢, $1, $3 and $5. The valley notes were signed by Brigham Young, Heber C. Kimball, Thomas Bullock and stamped with the official seal of the Twelve Apostles. Like, Valley Notes. Ohm'God.

What do the initials stand for on the valley notes?

PSTAPCJCLDSLDATW: Private Seal of the Twelve Apostles, Priests of The Church of Jesus Christ of Latter-day Saints, in the Last Dispensation All Over the World.

Turning the notes over reveals additional initials LYMIBKBB. These stood for "Love You, Mean It, Big Kiss, Bye-Bye." OK we made that last part up.

The first gold coins were dated 1849 and issued in a $10 denomination. Additional gold coins were later issued in $2½, $5, and $20 values.

What do the letters G.S.L.C.P.G. mean on the coins?

Great Salt Lake City Pure Gold.

Replicas of early Mormon money.

Was the money always backed by gold?

Nope. The Deseret Currency Association issued one of the more innovative monies. The currency was signed by Brigham Young and was backed by livestock. Written on the currency were the words, "Deseret Currency Association will pay the bearer…in livestock." They considered calling it "Moo-ney." Well, okay, they probably didn't, but we did.

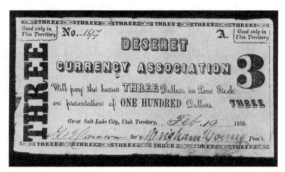

$3 Deseret Currency Association scrip note (typeset) courtesy Alvin E. Rust. From the book, "Mormon and Utah Coin and Currency."

The note pictured here was later shown to be a forgery, but since no actual $3 Deseret Currency Association notes are known to exist, we chose to use this picture to represent what it might have looked like.

The Church of Jesus Christ

What are the differences between the terms Mormons, Latter-day Saints, LDS, and The Church of Jesus Christ?

They are all separate descriptions for the same religion. It's like this: The official name is "The Church of Jesus Christ of Latter-day Saints." Latter-day Saints is sometimes abbreviated as LDS. Acceptable shortened references include "The Church of Jesus Christ" or simply "The Church." But when referring to members of "The Church" the term "Latter-day Saints" is preferred, though "Mormons" is acceptable.

Where did the word "Mormon" come from?

It is a reference to the *Book of Mormon*; one of the religious books The Church of Jesus Christ is based upon.

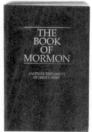

The Book of Mormon - Another Testament of Jesus Christ.

Why are there baptismal fonts in Church of Jesus Christ Temples? Can't a Mormon be baptized anywhere?

The living can, but not the dead. Another tenet of The Church of Jesus Christ faith is that God treats everyone alike, and the requirements for the dead and living are the same. Since the requirements of salvation include baptism, and the dead cannot be baptized personally, living people are "properly baptized for and on behalf of the dead."

Do Mormons really practice polygamy?

According to The American Heritage® Dictionary of the English Language, Fourth Edition *Polygamy* is defined as "The condition or practice of having more than one spouse at one time. Also called **plural marriage.**"

They did originally, but Church president Wilford Woodruff banned the practice in 1890. Maybe he realized that one nagging wife was more than enough. He issued a press release known as the "Manifesto" stating "I publicly declare that my advice to the Latter-day Saints is to refrain from contracting any marriages forbidden by the law of the land." Polygamy was proving to be the most contentious issue in Utah's bid for statehood. Woodruff's press release was approved at The Church's general conference on October 6th, 1890.

Did polygamy end with the Manifesto?

Not really. Church President Joseph F. Smith issued a "Second Manifesto" on April 7th, 1904. It allowed The Church to take action against people who still participated in plural marriages. In 1909 a committee of Church of Jesus Christ apostles investigated post-Manifesto polygamy and by 1910 put a new policy in place. Anyone who was involved in a plural marriage after 1904 was excommunicated and those married between 1890 and 1904 could not have Church callings where other members would have to sustain them. Despite all the prohibitions there are still practicing polygamists in Utah, but they are not approved in any way, shape or form by The Church of Jesus Christ.

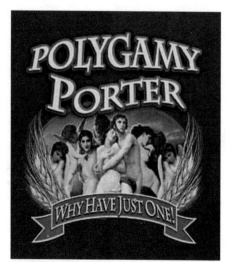

The only legal polygamy, "Polygamy Porter" from Wasatch Beers. Photo courtesy Greg Schirf of Wasatch Beers.

So, there's no polygamy?

The only legal polygamy is the 5.5% alcohol beer *Polygamy Porter*, brewed by Wasatch Beers in Park City. The brewery sparked controversy in late 2001 when it unveiled the beer and its advertising campaign. The campaign's billboards, which included such slogans as "Take one home for the wives" and "When enjoying our flavorful beverages please procreate responcibly," were rejected by Reagan Outdoor Advertising on the grounds that they were in bad taste.

Company owner Greg Schirf replied, "We've exhibited much worse taste than this." Previous campaigns have included slogans such as "Baptize your taste buds" and "Serving the local faithful."

Even avowed polygamists took offense, such as Owen Allred, leader of the nation's second-largest polygamist church, Apostolic United Brethren. He resented that something as natural and wholesome as polygamy would be affiliated with a practice as deviant as drinking beer.

Beehive Clothing Garment top.

The clergy and faithful of many major religions wear special clothing, but it's all external. The Church of Jesus Christ has no professional ministry and members wear their clothing under street clothes.

Do Mormons really marry for eternity?

According to The Church of Jesus Christ, "Civil marriage is an earthly contract, completed in the death of either party. Eternal celestial marriage is a sacred covenant between man and woman, consecrated in the holy temple by servants of God who hold authoritative keys. It bridges death; it includes both time and eternity." This ceremony is performed in "sealing rooms" in Temples. It makes the now-defunct doctrine of polygamy seem like a pretty good idea. Why put all your eggs in one basket?

Why is Utah sometimes called "land of the funny underwear?"

The term refers to the sacred garments worn by Church of Jesus Christ members who have received the ordinance of the temple endowment. Anyone who enters a Church of Jesus Christ Temple is required to wear the garments. Once a member makes the covenants of righteousness the garments are worn under their regular clothing for the rest of their lives.

The garments are "an outward expression of an inward covenant" to remind members of the sacred covenants they have made with God and "a symbol of the modesty of dress and living that should characterize the lives of all the humble followers of Christ."

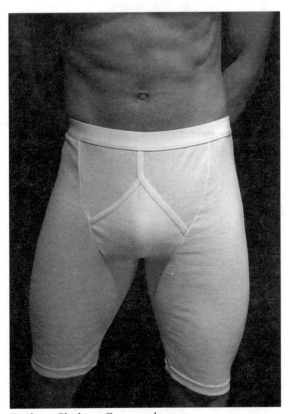

Beehive Clothing Garment bottom.

What do the garments look like?

Underwear. (See previous page.) They look like designer underwear from today's fashion houses. The only differences are "several simple marks of orientation toward the gospel principles of obedience, truth, life and discipleship in Christ."

Has The Church ever considered opening a fashion house? How about *The Shop of Christian Dior for Latter-day Saints*?

Well, they did, but it was a more lawsuit-free version. Brigham Young started the ZCMI (Zions Co-operative Mercantile Institution) in 1868. It was the oldest department store chain in the United States., and the largest in the state of Utah. The Church of Jesus Christ sold it in 1999 to the May Company for $52 million. For the first time, the stores opened on Sunday for business, except for the original location down the street from the Salt Lake Temple. The company continues to offer missionary discounts.

Facade of the Zions Co-operative Mercantile Institution (ZCMI) in Salt Lake City.

What do Mormons consider all non-Mormons to be?

Mormons consider people of any other religion to be "gentiles." Utah is probably the only place in the world where Jews are considered to be gentiles.

Is it true the founder of The Church of Jesus Christ Joseph Smith and the first President Brigham Young had navy ships named after them?

They sure did. The U.S.S. Brigham Young was a Liberty Class Merchant Ship that was christened on August 17, 1942. On May 22, 1943 another Liberty Ship was launched with the name U.S.S. Joseph Smith.

Did you ever wonder what U.S.S. means in the names of ships?

We did. United States Ship. Seems sort of obvious, doesn't it?

Why do some ships have SS in front of their name?

The SS stands for *Steam Ship* and was used in the full name of the steam powered Liberty Ships.

Liberty Ship SS Jeremiah O'Brien. Photo used by permission, National Liberty Ship Memorial, photo by Don Maskell, all rights reserved.

Politics and War

How did the Mexican War help determine where the Mormon settlers would migrate?

United States President James Polk asked The Church of Jesus Christ for a battalion of men. Five hundred volunteers were recruited and the Mormon Battalion was formed. This band forged a wagon route across the extreme southwest and marched 2000 miles to San Diego. The Battalion arrived after the war was over and fought only one battle - with a herd of wild bulls. The $70,000 pay they received and explorations completed helped the Mormon immigrants by financing them and aiding them in mapping out the best places to settle.

Monument to the Mormon Battalion at the Utah State Capitol building.

Who owned the state of Utah?

Other than the native Indians the first Europeans to *lay claim* to Utah were from Spain. Spanish explorers had arrived at the southern border of Utah as early as 1540 and two Franciscan priests, Dominguez and Escalante, traversed the Uinta Basin, crossed the Wasatch Mountains and visited the Indian encampment at Utah Lake in 1776.

In 1821 Utah became a part of Mexico after the Mexican independence from Spain. It remained under Mexican control until the Treaty of Guadalupe Hidalgo in 1848. That treaty ended the Mexican War and Utah became part of the United States.

Utah justice was called "mountain common law." What was that?

A brand of extra-legal violence that was carried out against the seducers of women and generally condoned in early Utah. A classic example occurred in February of 1851. Dr. John M. Vaughn allegedly had an affair with Madison Hambleton's wife while Hambleton was away working. Dr. Vaughn was warned his life would be in danger, but still the affair persisted, even after Mr. Hambleton returned.

On a Sunday afternoon, after Church meetings, Hambleton shot and killed Vaughn. Hambleton then immediately turned himself over to authorities and was escorted to Salt Lake City. Brigham Young represented him and he was acquitted. This severe brand of justice would continue for several years and newspapers of the day would publish editorials on the "inviolability of virtue."

How did Brigham Young deal with the Indians who lived in Utah?

Brigham Young made friendly overtures to the Indians believing it was, "…cheaper to feed them, than to fight them." However, that friendly attitude wasn't always the rule. In 1850 settlers at Fort Utah were complaining about raids on livestock and asked Brigham Young for justice. Young ordered a "selective extermination campaign" against the Timpanogos Utes. He stated that, "All the men were to be killed. The women and children were to be saved, only if they behave[d] themselves."

Were there any wars with Indians?

Several. The first was the Walker War with the Ute Indians. The Mormons had worked out compromises with the Paiutes but were occupying lands the Utes used for hunting and gathering. The Mormons were also disrupting the Utes' New Mexican trade in Indian slaves. On July 17, 1853 at the home of James Ivie several Utes were negotiating trades. A dispute arose and Ivie ended up killing one of the Utes named Shower-Ocats. Several more deaths followed on both sides until an uneasy peace was negotiated on May 11, 1854. Unfortunately none of the issues that had started the hostilities were resolved.

Additional battles erupted in the Tintic War after a Ute sub-chief and his fellow tribesmen began taking cattle from the settlers. They weren't taken for profit, but because there was a drought and the Indians were starving. More clashes and deaths followed.

The most serious was the Black Hawk War of 1865 to 1868 where more than 70 people lost their lives.

The federal government eventually moved the Utes to the Uintah and Ouray Reservation in the Uinta Basin during the late 1860s and early 1870s. However, the Utes never sold their lands and the issue remained alive until after World War II when the Indian Claims Commission ordered payment for confiscated lands.

Did Utah become a state after the Mormon settlers arrived?

Nope. Mormon settlers formed a political government and created the State of Deseret in 1849 and 1850. Unfortunately congress wouldn't admit Deseret to the Union and instead created the Territory of Utah, an area that until the 1860s encompassed most of present-day Nevada and parts of present-day Wyoming and Colorado.

Why the name Deseret? What does it mean?

Deseret is a word from *The Book of Mormon* that means honeybee. A beehive is the state symbol and stands for hard work, energy and industry, all part of a philosophy of life the early pioneers believed in. To this day beehives can be seen on everything from the state seal and flag, to fence posts and sidewalks.

A beehive at the State Capitol building, on the sidewalk and a fence post in downtown Salt Lake City.

Was there a flag for the State of Deseret?

Two possibilities have emerged. One was described by Dan Maguire as a flag hanging in the second floor window of Church of Jesus Christ President Heber C. Kimball's home in 1877 on the morning of Brigham Young's funeral.

It was described as, "…a flag having in its upper left hand corner a blue field with a circle of 12 stars and in the center a large white star. The stripes on that flag, instead of being red and white stripes, were blue and white stripes, and it was to be the flag denoting Mormon sovereignty."

One of two flags that could have flown over the State of Deseret.

The second appeared in 1880 at the General Conference during The Church of Jesus Christ's celebration of its 50th birthday. John D. McAllister, president of the Saint George Stake, saw the flag and described it in his journal.

"Fifty years today since The Church…was organized. Flags and banners unfurled. On the temple was a white one with a blue field, a circle of 12 stars and three in the center, in the form of a triangle, all representing the First Presidency and the Twelve, truth, peace and fidelity."

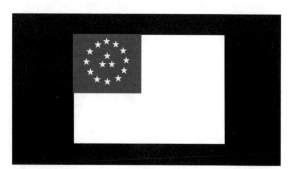

The second of two flags that could have flown over the State of Deseret.

What was the Utah War?

It was a disaster brought about by politics and failed communications. In the United States presidential election of 1856 national attention was focused on Utah as Republican candidates denounced the Mormon practice of polygamy.

In 1857 James Buchanan was elected President of the United States and he decided to find a non-Mormon governor for Utah. Buchanan and his cabinet believed the Mormons would violently resist the replacement of then Governor Brigham Young, so Buchanan sent a military force to Utah led by Albert Sidney Johnston. Buchanan also cancelled Utah's contract for mail service. No more junk mail, that would show them!

Since Governor Brigham Young wasn't given formal notification of Buchanan's intentions he interpreted the army coming as religious persecution. Young declared martial law and deployed the local militia to delay the troops. He also began something known as the "Move South." Church settlements in northern Utah were abandoned and prepared for burning. Approximately 30,000 people moved to Provo and other towns in central and southern Utah.

President Buchanan responded by appointing two commissioners, Lazarus Powell and Ben McCulloch to carry an amnesty proclamation to the Mormons. A deal was worked out between Governor Young and President Buchanan, the Utah war ended.

Were there any casualties in the Utah War?

Unfortunately yes, in a terrible incident known as the Mountain Meadows Massacre.

Four days before the massacre a rider was dispatched to Salt Lake City to ask Governor Brigham Young for advice on what to do with a group of emigrants who were passing through. The pioneers, caught up in an atmosphere of war hysteria, never waited for a reply and proceeded to kill between 100 and 150 California-bound emigrants at Mountain Meadows.

Two days later the answer from Young arrived. He said the pioneers should let the wagon train pass, and not to molest them. Fearful of repercussions the pioneers began an elaborate cover-up. The remains of the victims were thrown into shallow depressions and ravines, the bodies were covered with whatever was available and the episode was blamed on the Indians.

Only one man, John D. Lee, Major of the Fourth Battalion of the militia at Harmony was ever brought to justice. Lee was convicted and executed at the siege site of the Mountain Meadows Massacre on the 23rd of March, 1877.

When did Utah become a state?

January 4, 1896 Utah became the 45th state and Heber M. Wells was inaugurated as the first governor.

Portrait of Utah's first Governor Heber M. Wells at the City County Building in Salt Lake City.

But winning statehood was quite a fight. One of the principal points of contention was the Mormon practice of polygamy or plural marriage. The Church of Jesus Christ publicly acknowledged the doctrine of plural marriage in 1852 and that doctrine would provide the crucial stumbling block to statehood for the next four decades.

In 1862, just ten years after the doctrine of plural marriage was made official, Congress passed the Morrill Act prohibiting plural marriage in the territories. It also disincorporated The Church of Jesus Christ and restricted The Church's ownership of property. Since the nation was in the midst of a civil war the Morrill Act was not generally enforced.

In 1867 the Utah Territorial Legislature asked Congress to repeal the Morrill Act. They should have left it alone. The House Judiciary Committee instead questioned why the law was not being enforced and passed additional laws to strengthen the Morrill Act.

Seal of the State of Utah, with the year Utah became a state (1896) and the year the Mormon Settlers first arrived in the Salt Lake Valley (1847).

How did polygamy and a failed political maneuver help women get the vote?

In an attempt to solve "the polygamy problem" Senator Julian of Indiana suggested women in the territory of Utah should be granted suffrage. Anti-polygamy forces convinced him that if given a chance the "downtrodden and oppressed" women in Utah would rise up and vote to end plural marriage. Of course women weren't being oppressed and the Utah legislature knew they would provide a powerful voting force.

On January 11, 1870 the legislative assembly of Utah passed a bill granting the elective franchise to women. Acting Governor S.A. Mann signed it into law February 12, 1870.

Were Utah women the first in the United States to get the right to vote?

No, they were second. Wyoming passed a women's suffrage act in 1869, but Utah held the first election in which women voted. On the 14th of February the first woman to legally vote in an election in the United States was Sara Young, grand-niece of Brigham Young.

It is important to note that even though women had the right to vote, they still didn't have the right to hold an elected office.

Why did women later lose the vote?

The Edmunds-Tucker bill was passed by the United States Senate on January 12, 1886 and when finally approved in February 1887 became law. Among other things, the ruling abolished women's suffrage in the Utah territory.

It wasn't until Utah finally became a state in 1896 that women's suffrage was written into the state's constitution.

How tightly did The Church of Jesus Christ control politics in the state of Utah?

Until 1870 there were no opposing political parties in Utah. There was only the People's Party that was controlled by The Church. One set of candidates selected by Church authorities would appear on the ballot. Votes were limited to "yes" or "no." The ballots were numbered so it was possible to find out who voted and how. It was believed opposition was a tool of the Devil and that it would destroy orderly government.

This political control would remain until 1891 when The Church would dissolve the People's Party in an attempt at rapprochement with the Federal Government of the United States. The Church then randomly divided the population between Democrats and Republicans. The division was usually arbitrary and took place in Sunday meetings and other Church gatherings. People sitting on one side of the room were directed to be Democrats and people on the other were to be Republicans. For the first time the population of Salt Lake City would follow national party lines.

Was this the end of the Federal Government's meddling in the affairs of Utah?

Once Utah became a state there wasn't much interference for the next 30 years. The Federal Government primarily released "Farmers' Bulletins." Our favorites include, "Housecleaning Made Easier," "Ice Creams Frozen Without Stirring" and "Corn Meal as a Food and Ways of Using it."

Farmers' Bulletins from the United States Department of Agriculture.

Liquor laws seem a little different in Utah. For example, why can't I order a drink with a double shot in it?

You've run into one of the many unusual liquor laws in the state of Utah. According to the law no more than one ounce of primary liquor may be served to a customer. The law also says you can't have more than one drink in front of you at a time.

Fortunately for drinkers there are loopholes. Order a sidecar and your server or bartender will give you a second glass with a shot in it, and you can then mix your own double.

If I can only get a drink with a one-ounce shot how do I order a Long Island Iced Tea?

The additional liquors are "flavorings." We're not kidding! So be sure to practice the following sentence: "But officer, I only had five flavorings..."

What other unusual laws are there about liquor?

- Restaurants can serve beer and liquor but it must be consumed at the restaurant and you must also order food. (Do pretzels count?)
- You can buy 3.2 percent beer from grocery and convenience stores, but wine and spirits are only available at state liquor stores.
- You can drink alcohol without purchasing food at *private clubs*, but you must purchase a membership, ask a member on-site to sponsor you or buy a visitor pass.
- Taverns, also called brew pubs or beer bars, serve beer to be consumed on-site and you don't have to buy food or a membership.

And our personal favorite...

- Nobody in a private club can "encourage or permit any person to touch, caress, or fondle the breasts, buttocks, anus or genitals of any other person." We're not kidding!

Who was the first bar owner in Utah?

Brigham Young, but not because he was a supporter of alcohol. The bar room was opened primarily for travelers. Mormons believed someone would supply the need so better they control it than others.

Didn't Mormons also make alcohol?

Yes, but it was mainly for bathing, pickling (food, not themselves) and medicinal purposes. Very little was used for consumption.

How did Utah get so many unusual liquor laws?

Many of them began with the Utah prohibition on August 1, 1917 when the entire state of Utah went dry. Almost three years later, January 16, 1920, the 18th Amendment to the Constitution would pass imposing Prohibition nationwide. These laws brought Utah (and the nation) the speakeasy, bootleggers and thousands of illegal stills.

Lawmakers soon realized that Prohibition was a loosing battle and that if properly regulated the State of Utah could make money from liquor rather than spend money trying to enforce the unenforceable. Attempts began to have Prohibition repealed and laws put into place that would give the state more control. It would take 13 years and another Amendment to the

Constitution before it finally happened.

The 21st Amendment, repealing Prohibition, required ratification by 36 states to pass. Utah was the 36th due to Governor Blood's quick action in convening the legislature. On the 5th of December 1933, Prohibition was lifted nationwide. Ironically Utah remained a dry state until 3.2 beer became legal in January of 1934, and hard liquor wasn't legalized until the present state-run liquor store monopoly was established in 1935. Funny how many things are deemed immoral until our government figures out how to profit from them.

What was Commercial Street known for?

Saloons, gambling dens and brothels. Although gambling and brothels were prohibited by state law, business was booming on this narrow thoroughfare called Commercial Street, one block long, that ran between 100 and 200 South.

It was felt prostitution could not be eliminated, merely controlled. By confining it to "red-light districts" it could be watched and regulated. This area near the central business district was well established within 20 years following Salt Lake's settlement.

By 1886 police were arresting a few dozen prostitutes, fining them a maximum of $50 each, giving them medical exams and then releasing them. As long as the women weren't plying "their trade so openly and brazenly as to offend the public eye" they could go about their business unhindered. Then again, if that many public eyes were going to be offended, where would the demand for services be?

By 1908 the system was even more controlled with the police keeping track of the names and addresses of madams and the "girls" in their "houses." Basically, Salt Lake City was acting as their pimp. The women were expected to pay a monthly "fine" of $10 and they could continue with their business unmolested…so to speak. That year an average 148 women paid the fines each month and contributed $18,000 to Salt Lake City's general fund.

Brothels were so successful they had begun to grow beyond the bounds of Commercial Street. But this success would arouse public sentiment and lead to a recommendation by Chief of Police Thomas D. Pitt in his annual report in 1907:

"This question [of prostitution] is certainly a question

hard to dispose of, and, being a necessary evil, there is only one way in which it can be successfully handled, which is as follows: Let the city set aside a piece of ground of sufficient size to accommodate several hundred of these prostitutes. Enclose same carefully with high fences; build cottages or houses to accommodate these inmates; charge them rent, license them and place them under control of the Police Department as to their safety and confinement, and to the Board of Health as to their cleanliness and sanitary conditions."

So as not to arouse concern over a hard question, his recommendation was accepted and in the spring of 1908 Salt Lake City began planning "the stockade." Apparently the city council wasn't satisfied with passively pimping and wanted to take on duties that bore strikingly similar job desccriptions to those of Madam and Dominatrix. One suddenly has the image of council meetings taking place in dungeons with bullwhip brandishing council members in full leather. Who says politics has to be boring?

The mayor and city council directed that an area be walled off with "cribs" and "parlor houses" within the enclosure. (What? No cage?) Prostitutes could work essentially unhindered within the confines of the block.

In 1908 Dora B. Topham, a.k.a. "Belle London" was asked by the mayor of Salt Lake City to build and operate "the stockade." Topham formed a corporation called the Citizen's Investment Company and through it purchased land in the interior of Block 64. Architect Lewis D. Martin drew up the plans, construction began in September 1908. The work was finished in just three months. Talk about quick erections.

Dora B. Topham a.k.a. "Belle London." Photo used by permission, Utah State Historical Society, all rights reserved.

Why were the brothels moved from Commercial Street to Block 64?

Because Mayor Bransford owned property across the street and as a public official, had to monitor the situation. Or maybe he just had a leather fetish. Of course the official explanations were that the new area was bordered on two sides by railroad tracks, and with the completion of tracks by the Western Pacific would be on three sides. It was on the dividing line between two school districts so children wouldn't have to walk by it on their way to and from school, and "We found that most of the better class of residents were leaving the area anyway, because of the influx of Italians and Greeks who live in that neighborhood." (Their quote, not ours.)

The experiment lasted for three years before Dora Topham announced she would close the stockade. Ms. Topham stated that her reasons were because "there is a strong public sentiment in favor of such a course."

Prostitution would continue operating throughout Salt Lake City, although with less control than the stockade had offered.

The only house of prostitution still remaining from Salt Lake City's early years.

By 1982 only three of the old houses of prostitution were standing at 165, 167 and 169 Commercial Street. By 2001 the street had been renamed Regent Street and only one building remained.

Were cigarettes once illegal in Utah?

They were. The original anti-smoking legislation was an 1896 law that forbade the sale of cigarettes and related products to minors. Admirable though it was, many groups felt this law didn't go far enough and that cigarettes should be outlawed entirely.

For the next 25 years groups such as the No-Tobacco League, the Clean Life Army of the Anti-Cigarette International League and the Women's Christian Temperance Union rallied against the "evil weed." One wonders what they would have called marijuana?

Their efforts were successful and on March 8, 1921 Governor Charles R. Mabey signed a law that said:

"An act making it unlawful to sell cigarettes and cigarette papers, to advertise cigarettes and cigarette papers, to permit minors to smoke in certain places of business [and] for any person to smoke in certain enclosed public places."

The anti-smoking law took effect June 7, 1921.

The law was derided in newspapers as far away as Boston and San Francisco as an infringement of personal liberty, back when it was still unusual to lose personal liberties.

Four prominent Utah businessmen were arrested for smoking after dinner cigars in the Vienna Café in Salt Lake City including Ernest Bamberger, who was the National Republican Committeeman and former senatorial candidate and A.N. McKay, manager of the *Salt Lake Tribune*. This action would ultimately prove the undoing of anti-smoking legislation.

With mounting negative publicity, sporadic enforcement and a change in public temperament, Senate Bill 184 was proposed to repeal cigarette prohibition.

On March 8, 1923 Senate Bill 184 was passed in the House and signed into law by Governor Mabey. The prohibition on adult smoking was over.

How much of the State of Utah is owned by the Federal Government?

Three fourths of Utah land is owned by the Federal Government.

When did Salt Lake City loose it's greatness?

On January 29, 1868 the name Great Salt Lake City was changed to simply Salt Lake City.

How did the Ku Klux Klan affect Christmas in 1922?

In 1922 Klan membership had been opposed at the Latter Day Saints General Conference and in the *Deseret News*. In June of that year the Salt Lake City commission unanimously passed an anti-mask ordinance aimed at curtailing Klan activity in the valley. When Christmas came around the law hit a rather unexpected target: Santa Clauses were forced to remove their beards and the Klan was to blame!

What was the covenant policy inserted into real estate contracts?

It was a policy that effectively prohibited black people from purchasing homes and other property. It began with a realtor in 1939 named Sheldon Brewster. He brought the Salt Lake City Commission a petition with one thousand signatures asking that black residents be restricted to living in one area of the city. Brewster further suggested that the ghetto should be located away from the City and County Building so that visitors to the city would not come in contact with black people. Couldn't they have just moved them to the same neighborhoods as the Greeks and Italians, since all the "better class of residents" had moved away?

The Salt Lake City Commission denied the petition. However, restrictive covenant policies were inserted into real estate contracts and did have the effect of limiting black ownership for a decade, until the policies were finally ruled unconstitutional. But, let the record show, the City Commissioners were not wearing masks.

Transportation and Engineering

Did the Mormon settlers really cross the country with handcarts?

They did. Many were too poor to afford the larger ox-drawn wagons, so they loaded only the supplies that were most essential, and pulled them in handcarts across the country to the Promised Land. Approximately 250 died on the 1,350 mile trek from Iowa City, Iowa, but nearly 3,000, mostly British converts, made it to the Salt Lake Valley. The entire journey took an average of 85 days for each traveler.

Handcarts like this were pulled by settlers immigrating to Utah.

What is at the Bonneville Salt Flats and what happens there?

It's a racetrack where almost every world record for automobile speed and endurance has been set. Today racing, tomorrow the world's largest margarita!

Entering the Bonneville Salt Flats.

Thousands of years ago salt was left behind at the Salt Flats as the waters of Lake Bonneville receded. The salt varied in thickness from skim to several feet. At the thickest part the Salt Flats are hard as concrete and smooth as a floor. An ideal surface for speed racing because there's plenty of space and nothing to run into if you lose control of your vehicle. Just think, thanks to the preservative properties of salt, you can live fast, die young, and leave a good-looking corpse even if it isn't found for a few months!

The Blue Flame, responsible for setting several land speed records on the Bonneville Salt Flats. Photo used by permission, Utah State Historical Society, all rights reserved.

Most of the year the Salt Flats are covered with a thin layer of water making things muddy and unusable. However, for about 3 months, from the end of August or September until about the end of November, the salt is "dry" enough with just the right amount of moisture to keep tires cool and lessen the dangers of blowouts at high speeds.

The first car to race at the Bonneville Salt Flats got a speeding ticket. That's true! Didn't he see the speed trap?

Are there still wagon tracks across the Salt Desert?

Yes, from people who crossed more than 100 years ago. The tracks of the infamous Donner-Reed party were still visible more than a century later.

Tracks left on the Salt Desert are visible more than 100 years later!

Wasn't there a railroad that led into Salt Lake City? Why didn't the Mormon settlers just use that?

There was eventually, but not in 1847 when the first Mormon settlers began to arrive. The transcontinental railroad wouldn't be built for another 20 years.

What's the story behind the transcontinental railroad?

In 1825 George Stephenson ran the first successful steam locomotive in England. Inspired by that accomplishment *The Emigrant*, an Ann Arbor, Michigan newspaper suggested a railroad to the Pacific. Without a railroad there were only two ways to cross the continent. One was by ship which meant a long, slow journey around Cape Horn or across the Isthmus of Panama. The second was on horseback or wagon over mountains and through deserts. Neither was an easy or cheap option.

In 1846 the "Oregon Question" was resolved when the Oregon Treaty was signed. Suddenly the state of Oregon was officially American territory and more settlers began moving west.

Then came the discovery of gold in California in 1848 and the admission of California to statehood in 1850. The population of the Pacific Coast was growing rapidly but transportation was still unreliable and dangerous.

The American Congress had additional reasons for wanting a railroad. They believed it would hasten the final subjugation of the American Indians and reduce the time and expense to the United States of transporting mail and government supplies.

When the Civil War broke out, the Union wanted to strengthen its bond with California to counter the threat of that state's secession. Plus the Pacific Coast seemed defenseless without a reliable means of transportation to reach it.

So how did the government react?

The same as it would today: They commissioned a study. In 1853 the Army Corps of Topographical Engineers were appropriated money "to ascertain the most practicable and economical route for a railroad from the Mississippi River to the Pacific Ocean."

Two northern and two southern routes were surveyed between 1853 and 1855. There was tremendous debate about the routes because whichever was chosen would bring immense political and economic benefits to the states it passed through. The Army Corps of Topographical Engineers concluded that the railroad could be built on any of the four routes, but along the 32nd parallel (in the southern states) would be the least expensive.

Which route did the railroad take?

None of them, and it was all because of an engineer who worked for the Sacramento Valley Railroad named Theodore D. Judah.

Judah had lobbied politicians, merchants and financiers in Washington and California to build a transcontinental railroad but hadn't made much headway. But his luck changed when he talked to four merchants in Sacramento named Leland Stanford, Collis P. Huntington, Mark Hopkins and Charles Crocker. Judah convinced them that not only could a transcontinental railroad be built, but also its builder would become rich and famous. On June 28, 1861 the four incorporated and became the Central Pacific Railroad Company of California.

The owners of the Central Pacific were based in Sacramento California, so that became the west coast terminus by default. The Civil War helped because now there were no Southerners to worry about opposing a northern route.

When did they begin construction?

Not for almost two more years, and it took an Act of Congress to enable them to do it. The Railroad Act of 1862 authorized the Union Pacific Railroad to build westward from the Missouri River to the California boundary or until it met the Central Pacific. It also allowed the Central Pacific (which already had a charter from California) to push farther east and connect with the Union Pacific.

The Central Pacific finally broke ground at Sacramento on January 8, 1863. Several months later, December 2, 1863 the Union Pacific also broke ground.

How did the railroad companies raise money to pay for such a massive undertaking?

Through the benevolence of the United States government. In the Railroad Act of 1862 the government paid the railroads in land grants. The railroads were given a 400 foot right-of-way through the public domain and 10 sections of land for every mile of track. The sections were alternate sections, 5 out of every 10 on each side of the track, or one-half the land in a belt 20 miles wide.

Subsidies were also paid for every mile of track. The railroads were paid $16,000 a mile east of the Rockies and west of the Sierra Mountains, $32,000 a mile between the mountain ranges and $48,000 a mile in the mountains. The payment wasn't cash though. It was a 6 percent, 30 year U.S. bond and the railroads had to repay the principal and interest at maturity. This subsidy was the first mortgage on the railroad.

However, neither company made much progress. War sent the price of materials soaring and made labor scarce. More than a year after the Central Pacific broke ground it had only laid rails 18 miles east of Sacramento. The Union Pacific hadn't laid a single rail. (What is especially ironic about this is that on April 28, 1869 the Central Pacific set a world record that stands to this day by laying 10 miles of track in a single day.)

The railroad builders were facing ruin. Once again the government came to their rescue. On July 2, the Railroad Act of 1864 was signed that reduced the right-of-way from 400 feet to 200, but it doubled the land grant and the government gave up its first lien on the railroad. The government authorized the companies, as they received government subsidy bonds, to issue equal amounts of their own 6 percent, 30 year bonds. Now the company bonds would be a first mortgage on the railroad and the government bonds became the second mortgage. Finally the railroads had all the money they needed. Plus, with the end of the Civil War they also had enough labor and material. They would now push ahead on a 10 year job that would only take 4 years.

Did the transcontinental railroad meet in Salt Lake?

It didn't, much to the disappointment of Brigham Young, the powerful president of The Church of Jesus Christ. The transcontinental railroad officially met at nearby Promontory Range, Utah and at 12:47 p.m. on May 10, 1869 the final spike was driven uniting rails from the east and west coasts.

Final spike? Wasn't it a golden spike?

There was a golden spike presented by David Hewes, the San Francisco construction magnate. It was engraved with the names of the Central Pacific Railroad directors and on the head, the notation "The Last Spike." There was another golden spike presented by the San Francisco *News Letter*; a silver spike brought by United States Commissioner J.W. Haines as Nevada's contribution and a spike of iron-silver-gold alloy brought by Governor A.P.K. Safford to represent Arizona. But none of these was driven into the rail. The last spike was completely ordinary and made out of iron.

Driving in the final spike. Photo used by permission, Utah State Historical Society, all rights reserved.

Who drove in the final spike?

Leland Stanford, President of the Central Pacific Railroad Company and Governor of California, made the first attempt. He missed it and hit the rail instead. Then Thomas Durant of the Union Pacific Railroad Company tried. He missed and almost hit his foot, which explains why they were upper management and not workers. It took the construction superintendents James H. Strobridge of the Central Pacific and Samuel B. Reed of the Union Pacific to finally drive the spike in. The spike was wired to a telegraph that sent the news to a waiting America, three dots, DONE.

Why didn't the railroad go through Salt Lake City?

Because the route would have had to cross the treacherous salt flats west of the city. A way around the north end of the Great Salt Lake was significantly easier, cheaper and faster. So Brigham Young organized his own Utah Central Railroad and connected Salt Lake City with the town of Ogden and the transcontinental railroad.

Did the railroad ever cross the Great Salt Lake?

It did at the Lucin Cutoff. When the transcontinental railroad was finished it was full of curves and steep grades that became bottlenecks for the entire line. Southern Pacific Railroad officials surveyed the lake and in March, 1902 began building a route directly across from Ogden to Lucin near the west Utah border. Construction to the shores on each end of the route was relatively simple, but the bridge across the water would prove to be much more difficult.

The original cutoff was primarily rock and gravel fill through shallow lake water, approximately 12 miles of trestle and a 600-foot bridge at Bear River Bay. The difficult part was the fill, as trainload after trainload of solid rock and gravel disappeared into the soft mud below the water. Poles (or piles) for the trestle had to be driven sometimes more than 100 feet deep through mud before solid footing was found. A total of 28,250 piles were driven before construction was completed in 1903.

The Lucin Cutoff shortened the trip by 43.77 miles and 7 hours! Wood used in the construction was from straight trees 100 to 150 feet in length and became "pickled" by the lake brine. The piles are just as strong today as when originally set in place. In the 1950s the trestle portion of the cutoff was replaced with a solid rock and gravel fill and Cannon Construction began salvaging and selling this very valuable wood. This was the first "railroad that went to sea." Just a few short years later another railroad would take away this title, but that's a story for another book in our series, *True Secrets of Key West Revealed!*

True Secrets of Key West Revealed! For the strange and unusual on the southernmost island.

I've heard the hearse in front of Disney World's Haunted Mansion carried the body of Brigham Young in his funeral. Is that true?

That's just an urban legend. There was no hearse used in Brigham Young's funeral as pallbearers carried his coffin. The hearse is just a prop.

Allen Woods (True Secrets of Researcher) in front of the Walt Disney World Hearse in Orlando Florida.

Did Salt Lake City have a company that made electric cars?

Yes, the Whitmore Electric Automobile Factory was built in 1909. A. O. Whitmore came to Utah in 1894 to help develop the Nunn's Park Power Plant at the mouth of Provo Canyon. It was the first power station in the nation built for long-distance transmission of high-voltage electricity.

The A. O. Whitmore Electric Automobile Factory as it appears today in Salt Lake City.

Deciding to capitalize on his experience with electricity, Whitmore's factory built, sold and serviced electric automobiles until 1920. The factory was located strategically on South Temple to be near the wealthy families who could afford his vehicles. Whitmore stopped making electric cars in 1920 because of the enormous popularity of gasoline powered cars.

What did Daniel C. Jackling create in Bingham canyon that can now be seen from space?

The Utah Copper Company, the first open pit mine in the world. Daniel Jackling believed that open pit mining and mass production of low grade porphyry copper ores was not only possible, but also profitable. Most people thought he was crazy trying to mine ore that contained only .6% copper, but through large scale processing and by moving tons of material efficiently he was successful beyond most people's wildest dreams.

Today "The Pit" is officially called the Kennecott Bingham Canyon Mine and measures more than 2.5 miles across. At three quarters of a mile deep it could hold two Empire State Buildings standing on top of each other. It is the largest man made excavation on earth.

The mine grew so big it swallowed up the towns of Lark and Bingham. Over the mines' nearly 100 year history more than six billion tons of material have been mined and more than 16 million tons of copper metal have been recovered. More than two thirds of all Utah mineral production has come from the Kennecott Bingham Canyon Mine. Daily more than 500,000 tons of material is excavated.

The Kennecott Bingham Canyon Mine. That small speck is a dump truck with tires more than 12 feet tall!

Are there any other minerals removed from "The Pit?"

Gold, silver and molybdenum (a metal used to strengthen steel). Over the lifetime of "The Pit" the Kennecott Corporation has removed 21 million ounces of gold, 185 million ounces of silver and 740 million pounds of molybdenum. The cumulative value of the minerals removed from "The Pit" far exceeds the yields of the Comstock Lode, Klondike and California gold rushes combined!

Is Daniel Jackling related to Jack Daniels?

No, and now that we think about it, what a shame. Just imagine... Jackling could dig the holes and Daniels could fill them.

Is it true that the Kennecott Bingham Canyon Mine and the Great Wall of China are the only two man made objects that can be seen from space?

Nope. Even though it says that on a Trivial Pursuit card it's still wrong. Many man made things can be seen from space. (Of course by "space" we mean the "orbit" that an astronaut is in from 100 to 200 miles up.) You can see canals, highways, bridges, anything that's long and straight. The majority of natural features on the earth are irregular so the straight ones stand out.

Are they the only man-made objects you can see from the moon?

Wrong again. All you can see from the moon is clouds, water, deserts and vegetation. You can't make out any detail at all.

Were minerals discovered in other places around the Great Salt Lake?

Several places. In the 1880's copper and silver were even discovered *in* Salt Lake, on Antelope Island. Several mining companies were formed and 50,000 shares of the Great Lake Mining Company were sold. The ore was assayed and came back a rich 26% copper (versus the .6% at the Kennecott Mine). Unfortunately the rich veins came to an end nearly as quickly as they appeared and nothing much now remains except a few hundred holes in the ground.

Earth as seen from space. Photo courtesy National Aeronautics and Space Administration.

Buildings and Landmarks

What's the Beehive House?

It was Brigham Young's home in Salt Lake City. Next door is another former residence of his called the Lion House. For a further explanation of the Beehive phenomenon, see page 17.

The Beehive House.

The Lion House.

What's that big eagle doing over the road next to the Beehive House?

That's Eagle Gate, the original entrance to the Brigham Young property. The current gate bears only slight resemblance to its predecessors after the older, narrower gate was severely damaged by a truck in 1960. Brigham Young's grandson, George Cannon Young, designed the current gate. The copper eagle on top weighs two tons and has a wingspread of 20 feet.

The Eagle Gate.

What's that dark, gothic looking building across from Eagle Gate? It looks like the Addams Family winter cottage.

It's the Alta Club, an exclusive group founded in 1883 by Utah businessmen involved mostly in the mining industry. The first members were all non-Mormons and officially excluded Mormons from becoming members. It wasn't until after the turn of the century that the Club began admitting Mormons and later women. In what may be a case of too little, too late, The Church of Jesus Christ has erected large buildings around the Alta Club, keeping it in the shadows most of the day. Hey, don't mess with the Mormons.

Does the Brigham Young Monument have Brigham Young with his hands reaching out to Zion Bank?

That's the way it appears, but that's not what was intended. The statue was first displayed at the 1893 Chicago World's Fair and then placed at Temple Square. The outstretched hand was a symbol of reaching out to the people, not a bank's money. It was merely a coincidence that Zion Bank was built directly across from the famous statue.

On the side of the statue is a list of the names of everyone who accompanied Young into the valley. Included are 140 free men, three women, two children and three black slaves, although the slaves are listed with the more neutral phrase "colored servants."

They didn't use marble or oak! White pine was the primary building material available so the pioneers painted the pine columns to look like marble. The benches were painted with feathers and fingers to look like oak. Even the pipes of the organ are pine, painted to look like metal.

Brigham Young Monument at Temple Square, Salt Lake City.

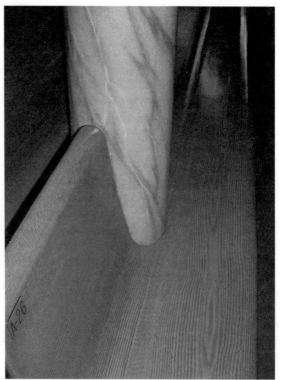

The Tabernacle's benches and columns painted to look like marble and oak. Temple Square, Salt Lake City.

What's the story behind the Tabernacle in Temple Square?

The Tabernacle was begun in 1863 and was the first building completed on Temple Square in 1867. The roof rests like an enormous inverted bowl on 44 columns of cut sandstone. Built without the use of a single nail, it's an incredible engineering feat. The people who built it were still living in log cabins and plowing with oxen.

Henry Grow originally supervised the construction but later Truman O. Angell was brought in to fix problems with the building's acoustics. After the addition of the gallery in 1870 the building became nearly acoustically perfect. The acoustics are so good you can hear a hairpin drop onto the floor from 200 feet away.

Where did all the marble and oak used in the Tabernacle construction come from?

How many pipes does the organ of the Tabernacle have?

Approximately 11,613 pipes, give or take a couple. (The editors chose to take a couple. They look fabulous in the den.)

Tabernacle organ in Temple Square, Salt Lake City.

How long did it take to build the Salt Lake City Temple?

Forty Years! The area where the Temple is located was dedicated in February of 1853 in a sacred service. April 6, 1853 the cornerstones of the building were laid and the capstone was laid on the 6th of April 1892. The completed temple was dedicated one year later.

The Salt Lake Temple is the most visited religious destination in North America.

The Salt Lake Temple.

Was the Temple once hidden?

Yes, in 1857, during the "Utah War" when Johnston's army was approaching Salt Lake City. The excavation and masonry foundation were covered up and the earth plowed to give the appearance of a cultivated field. Workmen re-excavated the foundation and resumed construction in 1858 when peace was restored.

Why can't I go inside the Salt Lake City Temple of The Church of Jesus Christ?

Only members of The Church of Jesus Christ in good standing are allowed inside because "the ordinances of the temple are so sacred that they are not open to the view of the public." Mormons who have what is called a *recommend* from their Bishop or Stake President and have a valid reason to enter are allowed inside. To get a *recommend* an interview is conducted to determine the following:

1. Do you have testimony of the gospel?
2. Do you support local and General Authorities?
3. Do you accept and follow the teachings and programs of The Church?
4. Do you keep the Word of Wisdom, including abstention from the use of harmful drugs?
5. Are you morally clean?
6. Are you a member in good standing in The Church?
7. Are you free from legal entanglements?

But you can *see* what the temple looks like inside, and it's all because of a less than legitimate promoter and 68 "stolen" pictures.

It all began on a Saturday morning the 16th of September 1911. The *Salt Lake Tribune* headline read, "Photographs secretly taken of Mormon Temple's interior…"

A man named Max Florence had, over a period of several months, snuck into the Salt Lake City Temple and clandestinely took photographs. There were pictures of "furnishings and adornments of every room in the magnificent edifice, together with reproductions of marriage records and minute books of many important meetings held by the Quorum of the Twelve Apostles and First Presidency, running back over a considerable period."

When the story broke, Florence was in New York City offering his pictures for sale to "the highest bidder." He even wrote to the First Presidency of The Church of Jesus Christ offering the views "for sale." The Church President replied with the statement "Church will not negotiate with thieves and blackmailers."

Florence got into the Temple with the help of Gisbert Ludwig Gerhart Bossard. He was a Swiss convert to The Church of Jesus Christ but had a falling out with The Church and wanted to "get revenge." Bossard befriended an assistant gardener at the temple named Gottlieb Wuthrach. Wuthrach had keys to the Temple and gave Bossard and Florence access to take the photographs.

To reduce the negative impact the sensationalistic press reports might have, University of Utah professor James E. Talmage proposed a solution. Six days after the incredible headline appeared on the *Salt Lake Tribune* Talmage suggested that The Church publish an *authorized* book of photographs. The day after Talmage proposed it he received a letter from the First Presidency of The Church of Jesus Christ confirming his appointment to prepare the book. The famous photographer Ralph Savage (who was a member in good standing) was put under contract and work on the official book was begun.

Over the next several months Max Florence continued to try to sell his Temple pictures, but wasn't having much luck closing any deals. By the 13th of November he and Bossard rented the Bijou Theater in Manhattan and planned a "sensational exposé." Unfortunately for Florence and Bossard, New York newspapers refused to carry stories about the show's opening and turned down their advertising.

The show was a disaster. Only two people were in the audience at the beginning. As the show went on only six more went in. In Bossard's lecture he claimed to have crawled through underground tunnels to enter the Temple (he walked in the door with a key) and displayed several photographs that were obvious fakes, including some drawn by local newspaper cartoonists! Bossard didn't speak English very well and his delivery was considered unintelligible. For subsequent shows Bossard was replaced with a professional lecturer.

It was a quirk of fate that just two days before Bossard and Florence's show the Mormon Tabernacle Choir was in New York City and performed before a packed house in Madison Square Garden.

Soon Florence and Bossard would have a falling out, with Bossard sending a letter to the President of The Church of Jesus Christ Joseph F. Smith apologizing and asking for forgiveness.

Florence never managed to find a buyer for the photographs and within a few months The Church published Talmage's book on temples. The book was called *The House of the Lord* and subtitled *A study of Holy Sanctuaries Ancient and Modern* and *Including Forty-six Plates Illustrative of Modern Temples*.

The Church's photographs were copyrighted but made available to anyone who wanted to "legitimately" publish the LDS view of temples and their purposes.

Max Florence returned to Utah financially strapped. It would take Prohibition before he would get back on his feet again making and marketing illegal liquor.

Ironically for all the money Florence lost with his failed "secret temple photographs" he could easily have made it up with an offer he later received. An up and coming movie producer from New York City asked Florence to invest in a film studio somewhere in the West, possibly Salt Lake City. Florence turned him down. That movie producer was Cecil B. DeMille and the studio Mr. DeMille helped found was Paramount Pictures in Hollywood, California.

What's the Salt Lake City Temple made of?

White granite. The pioneers quarried the granite from Little Cottonwood Canyon twenty miles away and hauled it to Salt Lake City on ox-drawn wagons. Later a canal was dug to float the granite out, but digging stopped before many miles were completed upon news that a railroad would be built. During final stages of construction the granite was shipped out on railroad flatcars.

Little Cottonwood Canyon.

Who is that a statue of on top of the Salt Lake City Temple?

The angel Moroni. According to The Church of Jesus Christ, Moroni was an ancient prophet who appeared to Joseph Smith and began the process of restoring God's Church to the earth.

Do Mormons worship the angel Moroni?

Not at all. Moroni is a figure of respect, and now the

image of Moroni with a horn to his lips has become a symbol of efforts by the Mormons as they preach the gospel around the world.

The Angel Moroni on top of the Salt Lake City Temple.

What about Captain Moroni?

Captain Moroni is an action figure based on the person Moroni *before* he became an angel. Captain Moroni is made by a company called Latter Day Designs. Captain Moroni's Ferrari and beach house sold separately.

Captain Moroni doll by Latter Day Designs.

What was the first recycling project at Temple Square?

The Assembly Hall. Now used primarily as an annex for Church conferences it was built out of leftover granite from the Temple.

Why is there a Star of David in the rosette window of the Assembly Hall?

It reflects the Latter Day Saints affinity with Old Testament Judaism.

Didn't there used to be a hotel on Temple Square?

There was. Hotel Utah, known for 76 years as "the Grande Dame of Hotels" was recognized for its elegance and exceptional service. It was built for $2 million dollars and opened on the 9th of June, 1911. Famous guests have included John Kennedy, Katharine Hepburn and Liberace. In the 1970s the Hotel Utah underwent a massive remodeling originally budgeted at $6 million that ended up exceeding $15 million. The hotel was closed in August of 1987 because of a decline in business.

The former Hotel Utah. Today it is the Joseph Smith Memorial Building.

The Hotel's owner, The Church of Jesus Christ, initially didn't know what to do with the building. Running it as a hotel was an unnecessary drain on finances, but the community was asking for it to be kept as an historical landmark. A decision was made to convert it to offices, community meeting halls and a visitors center through "adaptive reuse."

The former hotel is now known as the Joseph Smith Memorial Building in honor of The Church of Jesus Christ Martyr and Prophet. Today the ground floor and mezzanine levels are beautifully restored and available for public use. Few remnants of the original furnishings of Hotel Utah remain except occasional ashtrays in antique stores.

Ashtray from the former Hotel Utah.

What's the best view in Temple Square?

From the top of the Church Office Building, Headquarters for The Church of Jesus Christ of Latter-day Saints. Take the elevators to the 26th floor observation deck and you are rewarded with a spectacular view of the Salt Lake Valley.

How come there are only women tour guides in Temple Square?

Men are seen as too intimidating.

Was the Salt Lake City Temple the first Church of Jesus Christ temple?

Nope. That would be one built in Kirtland, Ohio, dedicated in 1836. It is still standing today. Referred

to as a "preparatory temple" many sacred rites were revealed in this temple but it was abandoned as the Mormons were persecuted and driven out of Kirtland.

The Church of Jesus Christ Office Building.

Does The Church of Jesus Christ have a secret fortress in the mountains that border Salt Lake City?

Sort of, but it's not secret and it's not really a fortress. It's the Granite Mountain Records Vault of The Church of Jesus Christ of Latter-day Saints. Situated approximately 200 feet above Little Cottonwood Canyon road it's a catacomb of stone that reaches nearly 700 feet into the mountain.

Why was the vault built?

The Church of Jesus Christ is one of the world's leading organizations involved in genealogical research. In 1938 The Church began using microfilm and as the years went by their collection of film grew. By the 1950s they had amassed records on millions of individuals and needed a secure, climate controlled facility to house them.

In 1960 construction began with hard rock miners

drilling and blasting their way into the mountain. The vault was finished and opened in 1966.

Why aren't visitors allowed inside?

Visitors are allowed but the numbers are very limited to ensure that the climate controlled environment of the vault is maintained. Today the vault holds over 2.3 million rolls of microfilm and 180,000 sets of microfiche. New records are being added daily as information comes in from around the world.

If you are preparing to do genealogical research while in Salt Lake City don't go to the mountain. The Church of Jesus Christ has brought the mountain to you. You can visit the Family History Library in Temple Square and have access to the largest repository of genealogical records in the world.

Cathedral of the Madeleine.

Granite Mountain Record Vault. Photo used by permission, The Church of Jesus Christ of Latter-day Saints, all rights reserved.

Are there other great religious buildings in Salt Lake City?

Several, but one of the most impressive is the Catholic Church's Cathedral of the Madeleine. It is a massive building of brownish gray sandstone built in the Romanesque style. The Cathedral of the Madeleine has everything, gorgeous ornate stained glass windows, giant gothic towers and gargoyles.

Is there a Pyramid in Salt Lake City?

There is, called the Summum Pyramid. Built in 1979 as a sanctuary and temple, the pyramid is 40 feet wide at the base and 26 feet tall. According to the Summum website:

"Its large concrete foundation is aligned with true north of the Earth, allowing the sides of the pyramid to face the cardinal points of the universe. Within the apex and four corners of the pyramid rest large Brazilian quartz crystals. These crystals are cut in precise shapes and tuned (programmed) to specific frequencies. This creates a highly sophisticated resonant chamber which in turn energizes the pyramid through the operative Neter forces."

The pyramid stores the Summum *Nectar Publications* and is used as a classroom for people studying the Summum philosophy.

I've heard they sell wine in the Summum Pyramid, why?

For the Summums the creation of nectars (or wines) is a religion, so they take it very seriously. Local and federal authorities didn't acknowledge the making of wine "creation and use of the nectars" as a valid religious practice, so Summums were forced to license the sanctuary as a winery in 1980. Today vintages such as "Sexual Ecstasy" are available to members.

Do the Summums also make mummies?

They do. They are the only group in the United States that are able to and have performed mummification of cats, dogs and birds. Even people, who have made appropriate arrangements, can be mummified after their

The Summum Pyramid.

deaths. For more info, call 1-800-KING-TUT. (The phone number is a joke folks.)

"Once the body is mummified, it can be placed in a standard casket or sealed inside a 'Mummiform.' The Mummiform is a metal container, generally made of bronze, shaped like a body, with the face of the person whose body it holds, what Summum calls a 'life mask.' The Mummiform is welded shut and can be adorned with any decorations one would like on it."

-From the Summum website.

This is the place monument.

A giant monument was built to commemorate the arrival of Brigham Young into the Salt Lake Valley. Is that where Brigham Young said, "This is the place"?

Well, not exactly. The actual location was about 17 miles above the site of the present monument but it wasn't nearly as convenient to reach.

Brigham Young also never said "This is the place." He was sick with "tick" or "mountain fever" on July 24,

1847 when he entered the valley. Two days later he made an inspection and upon seeing an outcropping of rock that was the same as a vision he had had, Brigham Young stated, "It is enough. This is the *right* place. Drive on." So basically, the monument to The Right Place is in the wrong place, and the "right place" quote is the wrong quote.

To this day July 24th is celebrated as "Pioneer Day" and is a state holiday in Utah.

Why are the streets in Salt Lake City all so wide?

They were laid out to be 132 feet wide, so that an ox team could be turned around easily. The streets were run north-south and east-west, and each was named for its distance from the Salt Lake Temple. For example, Fourth South Street is the 4th street south of the temple and runs east and west. Specifying the locations by their relation to the temple made things uniform and emphasized the importance of religion in the city.

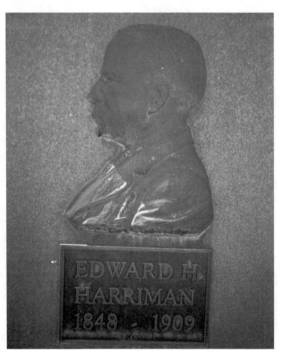

Railroad magnate E. H. Harriman relief at the Utah State Capitol building.

What helped finance the Utah State Capitol building?

Death and taxes. In 1911 the state of Utah collected a five percent inheritance tax from the estate of railroad magnate E. H. Harriman. The check came to a whopping $798,000. This was used as seed money to begin construction. The groundbreaking was on December 26, 1912 and the building was finally completed and dedicated October 9, 1916.

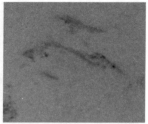

Marble faces of "Queen Elizabeth" and "Sparrow" in Utah State Capitol building.

Utah State Capitol building.

The Ionic columns that line the interior of the capitol are each carved from a single piece of marble and weigh 25,000 pounds. They are believed to be the largest solid marble columns in America.

What are a butterfly, Persian rug, hourglass, yawning lion and the heels of two socks together doing in the State Capitol building? It sounds like a yard sale that got out of hand.

They are designs that appear in the marble panels that line the walls. The panels are horizontally and vertically symmetrical and were created by slicing large blocks of marble and opening them up like a map. Names were later given according to the appearance the patterns made. Other two-dimensional residents include "Queen Elizabeth," "Satan" and "The Sparrow."

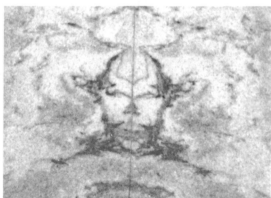

Marble face of "Satan" in Utah State Capitol building.

Is there really a room made entirely of gold in the State Capitol building?

Almost. *The State Reception Room* is more commonly called The Gold Room. The tables, chairs and ceiling are covered in 23-carat Utah gold. Even the mirrors were backed with gold instead of silver to remain consistent. The original cost of the furnishings was valued at about $65,000, but today they are valued at several million dollars. We thought they might have been remnants from Pimp of the Year contests held there. We were mistaken, but for more information on pimping in Salt Lake City, see page 21.

Marble columns inside the State Capitol building.

State Reception Room or "Gold Room" in the Utah State Capitol building.

Has the capital of Utah always been Salt Lake City?

No, the original capital was the town of Fillmore, chosen because of its central geographical location in the state. Unfortunately the town was too far away from the population center so the capital was eventually moved to Salt Lake City.

Where did Utah state senators meet before the State Capitol building was built?

The City and County Building. But construction went through several fits and starts before finally being completed.

The City and County Building.

The first site selected was at First South and Second East, but the County objected because the location was not close enough to the business center of town. After considering several other sites the corner of First South and First East was agreed upon. A competition was held for the architectural plans, architect C.E.

Apponyi won and construction began in autumn of 1890. The site was excavated, footings poured and nearly $20,000 of work completed before it was determined that the location had poor geologic conditions AND the building would be too large for the site.

After considering several more possibilities it was decided to start again at 8th Ward Square (known today as Washington Square). Once more a competition was held for architectural plans and that time the Salt Lake firm of Messrs. Monheim, Bird and Proudfoot was selected to be the new architect. The building was designed in the Richardson Romanesque style.

In December 1891 John H. Bowman began construction as low bidder at $377,978. Construction was again hampered by poor planning when quicksand was discovered under the soil. Trainloads of broken rock were dumped into the excavation and the entire 31,150 foot foundation had to be encased in concrete. Work stoppages, delays and problems continued until July 26, 1893 when Bowman was dismissed.

Now the City Council assumed all responsibility for completing the building. Cost overruns had become so great that in the spring of 1894 officials considered shutting down the entire project for lack of funds. Miraculously the needed construction bonds were sold, enough money was raised and in December of 1894 the building was finished at last. The final cost of construction was $892,534, more than double the original amount bid. When completed it was the most expensive building in Utah.

In 1895 Utah's constitutional convention was held there and for 20 years it served at the state's Capitol Building. Today it is the center of Salt Lake City and County governments.

What is Gilgal Garden?

It's the only "visionary art environment" in Utah. Thomas Child, who was without any formal training, began working in 1945 sculpting statues and pieces of art in Gilgal Garden. He was 57 years old at the time. For the next 18 years he went to incredible lengths to obtain huge stones, some weighing up to 62 tons, for his sculptures.

Child used an oxyacetylene torch to cut the rock and the process fused the remaining stone, giving it a polished sheen. There are 12 original sculptural

Joseph Smith Sphinx at Gilgal Garden.

arrangements and more than 70 stones engraved with scriptures, poems and philosophical texts. Child's sculptures include *The Sphinx,* which is built to look like the Sphinx in Egypt and has the face of Church of Jesus Christ founder Joseph Smith (nose intact). Another is *The Monument To The Trade* that is a self portrait of Mr. Child wearing brick pants. Oddly enough, even after Gilgal Garden was opened to the public, brick pants never caught on as a fashion phenomenon.

Thomas Child's self portrait at Gilgal Garden. Mr. Brick pants!

What is Saltair?

"The Lady of the Lake." A resort that in 1893 was built in six months and originally stood in thirteen feet of water. Saltair became the headquarters for activities on the Great Salt Lake including political campaigns, civic and cultural events.

The first Saltair was an architectural wonder with a Moorish flair. Designed by Richard K. A. Kletting the entire complex measured more than 1,100 feet from tip to tip. Three hundred tons of steel girders supported its dome and thousands of lights made the building a spectacle to behold at night. Everything was built to uplift and impress. Even the dance floor was huge and was advertised as the largest in the world.

Saltair opened to the public on Memorial Day in 1893 and was officially dedicated on June 8th.

The original Saltair. Photo used by permission, Utah State Historical Society, all rights reserved.

Did Saltair have its own railroad?

Yes. A railroad was built in 1893 to bring customers from Salt Lake City to Saltair. The original name was the Saltair Railway Company, but it was soon renamed the Salt Lake and Los Angeles Railway Company reflecting an intention to extend the line all the way to California. Roundtrip fare was fifty cents, which also paid for admission into Saltair. Unfortunately, ambition eclipsed action, and the railroad never went beyond Saltair.

Who owned Saltair?

The Saltair Beach Company built Saltair. The Church

of Jesus Christ owned half of the company's 2500 shares and the resort was built in an effort to provide a proper place of recreation for the entire family. The Church had been concerned about "pleasure resorts" and their harmful influence on young men and women. Saltair was built as a wholesome alternative.

To encourage a healthy environment Saltair Beach Company officials were not originally going to sell alcohol, but changed their minds before the resort opened. Company officials also decided to be open on Sundays, much to the distress of The Church of Jesus Christ.

How popular was Saltair?

The first year, 1893, Saltair had 100,000 paying visitors. That was when the entire population of Salt Lake City was less than 50,000!

Did The Church of Jesus Christ exert any influence over the resort?

Not much, only over the issue of alcohol. Throughout the 1890s the bar was periodically closed when Church of Jesus Christ groups had outings there. It wasn't until 1901 that Saltair's management decided to stop selling liquor entirely, but they did allow people to bring in their own alcohol.

The next year, in June 1902, the management of Saltair again decided not to sell "intoxicating drinks." The Church of Jesus Christ's Young Men's Mutual Improvement Association (YMMIA) and Young Women's Mutual Improvement Association (YWMIA) issued a statement urging "our membership, in all the stakes of Zion, to patronize Saltair with their pleasure excursions, in preference to other resorts where intoxicants are sold." Even the *Deseret News* said that Mormons had a "duty to themselves, to their families, and to the Church" to patronize Saltair. Saltair remained dry until 1904.

What did The Church of Jesus Christ do then?

They were caught in a dilemma. The Church could force the management company to go permanently dry, but people were bringing in their own liquor and getting more drunk than when it was regulated in the bar. The only reasonable alternative was for The Church to sell their interest in Saltair. In 1906 they sold their shares to a group of private individuals, including a Mr.

Langford, Charles W. Nibley, Joseph Nelson and Nephi W. Clayton. By this time attendance had grown to 250,000 annual paying visitors.

Is Saltair still operating on the Great Salt Lake?

Sort of, but it's not the original. On April 22, 1925 a workman smelled smoke from the Ali Baba Cave concession. Fire started, was put out, came back and within two hours the resort was destroyed. A burnt out mass of iron and smoldering beams was all that was left.

What did the owners do?

Why rebuild of course! But not before some of the businessmen who owned shares in the resort decided that would be a good time to divest those shares. On May 8, 1925, Saltair was offered to the City of Salt Lake as a gift.

It took the city commission three weeks to decide what to do and in the end they said "Thanks, but no thanks." The economics of running such a large resort that had to be rebuilt after a tragic fire, was far more than the city commissioners were willing to take on.

The second Saltair. Photo used by permission, Utah State Historical Society, all rights reserved.

When did Saltair reopen?

July 1, 1925, less than three months after the fire. There was still extensive damage and much of Saltair was closed off, but the resort was open for business.

In 1926 owners of the Salt Lake, Garfield and Western Railroad, Ashby Snow, David P. Howells and Willard T. Cannon purchased Saltair and announced they were going to build a new $350,000 pavilion.

The new pavilion was rebuilt along the same Moorish lines of the original, but bigger and better. The second Saltair was 100 feet longer and 15 feet wider, more spacious, elaborate and well appointed.

May 29, 1926 the second Saltair opened.

So the Saltair in operation today is the second one?

Nope, but you're getting warmer. Keep reading…

Didn't Saltair have a roller coaster?

It did and it was one of the largest in the West. Then on August 30, 1957 a freak 75 mile-per-hour gust of wind destroyed the giant coaster. A decision was made not to rebuild the racer. Saltair opened the next year but attendance was so low that on January 9, 1959 Ashby Snow gave the "Lady of the Lake" to the Utah State Parks and Recreation Commission. Saltair was closed, again.

What did the state of Utah do with it?

Absolutely nothing. As the years went by the windows were broken out, the wood deteriorated and the entire structure rotted. In 1970 a second devastating fire burned Saltair completely to the ground.

This time there would be no miraculous rebuilding. The state hadn't been able to do anything with it and nobody was sure they could make money with a Salt Lake resort.

Nobody except four businessmen, John C. Silver, James S. Silver, Wallace Wright and Stewart Grow. In an effort to recapture the popularity and charm of its predecessors they opened Saltair III. The pavilion was a 36,000 square foot abandoned airplane hangar from Hill Air Force Base. (Smith & Edwards, the local military surplus reseller, had stopped stocking hangars; they took up too much space in the aisles of the store.) A facade was built to resemble the original Saltair and in July of 1982 Saltair III was opened for business. Picture a box with some over-sized Hershey's Kisses on top, and that is the building known as Saltair.

The four businessmen of the apocalypse then entered the winter of their discontent, as the winter of 1982-1983 was the wettest in Utah's history. The water, which had been a quarter mile away when they opened, was now beginning to rise.

Saltair in 2001.

By the summer of 1984 the water was close to its historic high. The parking lot was inundated and there was 5 inches of water on the dance floor. Amazingly, the number of visitors was at an all-time high. Unfortunately, the clientele was comprised mostly of brine shrimp and their fly escorts. Saltair III was drowned out of business in less than 3 years.

In the fall of 1992 the Great Salt Lake Land Company bought the resort. The new owners restored the structure and added a concrete stage to present local and national artists. It was opened June 8, 1993, Saltair's 100th anniversary.

Today the Saltair resort is open but it's only a shadow of its former self. In fact, it wouldn't even fill the shadow of its former self, though perhaps that is how to see it in its best light. There are no trains, no rides, no changing rooms nor swimming suits for rent. There are a couple small gift shops, a snack bar and occasional dances.

The Salt Palace.

What is the Salt Palace?

The downtown Visitors and Convention Center. The original Salt Palace was built in 1899 and before completion the wood used in construction was sprayed with powdered salt under pressure to make the dome sparkling white. This led to the name "Salt Palace." It had an amusement park, roller coasters and the fastest bicycle track in the country. Unfortunately it burned down in 1910. The current Salt Palace has 365,000 square feet of continuous exhibit space and a 45,000 square foot ballroom. That's enough space for 2,900 ballerinas in tutus!

What did the Salt Lake Theater take in exchange for tickets?

The Salt Lake Theater opened in March of 1862. Money was scarce so tickets were exchanged for goods. Theater records show that one day's receipts included: 20 bushels of wheat, 5 bushels of potatoes, 4 of corn, 2 of oats, 2 hams, 1 pig, 1 wolf skin, 5 pounds of honey, 16 strings of sausage and 1 cat.

There was even a story of a young man on a date that gave the box office clerk a turkey and asked for two balcony seats. The clerk gave him the tickets and two spring chickens in change, which he then had to hold throughout the performance. No joke!

What are the giant balls floating in the desert?

[Ed. Note: Authors' commentary deleted for reasons of legality and propriety.]

That would be the Tree of Utah, next to the westbound lane of Interstate 80 approximately 26 miles east of Wendover and 75 miles west of Salt Lake City. It's a sculpture rising 87 feet high and visible from a distance of 17 miles. Utah Highway Patrol estimates that two million cars pass the Tree annually and five to seven cars an hour stop so occupants can get out to view it. Of course stopping to see it is a violation of the law since stopping along this highway is permitted only in cases of emergency.

The Tree was a dream of artist Karl Momen, a traveler through Utah who was so taken by the surreal nature of the scenery, while driving through the Salt Flats, that he was moved to create this sculpture. No public funds were used to create the Tree of Utah and it was undertaken at great personal expense to the artist and amid considerable controversy.

The Tree of Utah has been called everything from a "Vision in the Desert" to "Momen's Monumental Meatballs." The *Wall Street Journal* even carried a

headline that read "Sure, the Redwoods Grow Taller, But They Don't Have Coconuts."

In the end Karl Momen didn't want to load the Tree with too much meaning so he said simply "I don't want to be a messenger. I'm just an artist." Sure thing, Karl. Meaning and aesthetics are just too dogmatic.

The "Tree of Utah" rising 87 feet high in the middle of...nowhere.

Natural Wonders

How large is the Great Salt Lake?

Salt Lake is roughly 75 miles long and 50 miles wide with a surface area of approximately 1,500 square miles. It's the 33rd largest lake in the world but those dimensions are not static. The shores slope so gently that the rise of a few feet of water can add hundreds of square miles of lake surface. The Great Salt Lake is actually the largest body of water between the Great Lakes and the Pacific, and it's in the middle of a desert.

Has it always been about the same size?

Thousands of years ago the Great Salt Lake was part of a much larger body of water called Lake Bonneville. It was named after Captain Bonneville, an army officer who from 1832 – 1835 supposedly explored and reported on the lake's terraces. The fact is that Bonneville never set eyes on the Great Salt Lake.

In what could be called Exploration Outsourcing, he hired Joseph Reddeford Walker who did the exploring. It was, no doubt, neither the first nor last time an employer has taken credit for a temp's work. In 1837 Washington Irving published Bonneville's maps and journals in *The Adventures of Captain Bonneville in the Rocky Mountains and the Far West*. Bonneville's name would be immortalized. And the real explorer Joseph Reddeford Walker? Well at least you know now.

Lake Bonneville was 340 miles long and 145 miles wide. It was deepest where Salt Lake City is today,

over 1,000 feet. As far away as the city of Logan, water was 650 feet deep.

Were there actually plans to drain the lake?

There were. In 1873 a study was made to see if the lake could be drained into Nevada to get rid of it once and for all. It was determined not to be an economically worthwhile project at the time and Nevada didn't want it. Plus, there were fears that all that water would short out The Strip in Las Vegas. Nothing much happened until the winter of 1982 – 1983 when an incredibly wet winter brought the lake to the highest levels in recorded history. Parts of Salt Lake City were flooded or threatened and something had to be done.

Flooding in Salt Lake City, June of 1983 at State street and 800 South. Photo used by permission, United States Geological Survey, Salt Lake City, photo taken by Doyle Stephens, all rights reserved.

In 1986 the State of Utah began construction of a system to pump excess water west onto the Bonneville Salt Flats, creating the Newfoundland Evaporation Basin. A pumping station was built at Hogup Ridge, nearly 25 miles of dikes were put in place and a 37 mile natural gas pipeline to fuel the pumps was laid. In April 1987 the first pump was turned on and it moved 1.6 million gallons of water per minute! By June of 1989 the lake had declined nearly six feet from its peak and the pumps were finally turned off. Two feet of the decline was attributed to the pumping.

Shoreline of the Great Salt Lake.

Pump station at Hogup. Photo used by permission, United States Geological Survey, Salt Lake City, photo taken by George Pyper, all rights reserved.

Where does the water come from that fills Salt Lake?

The rivers Jordan, Bear and Weber are the source of almost half of Salt Lake's water. The remaining water comes from minor runoff, underground springs and rainfall. There is no output. Once water enters the lake its only means of escape is through evaporation, a process contributing to the salinity of the remaining water.

How deep is Salt Lake?

The deepest point is approximately 34 feet between the two islands of Antelope and Carrington. The average depth is approximately 13 feet.

How salty is the Great Salt Lake?

The water is actually one-fourth salt, making the Great Salt Lake the second saltiest body of water on earth. Only the Dead Sea is saltier. There is so much salt – nearly six times more than the ocean – it is nearly impossible for a swimmer to sink! Rumor has it that Jesus vacationed a lot in the Salt Lake City area, honing his aquatic skills.

What is it like to swim in the Great Salt Lake?

We think the experience was best summed up by two journalists more than 100 years ago. Fitz Hugh Ludlow in 1863 said that he felt "the pleasant sense of being a pickle, such as a self-conscious gherkin might experience." William Elkanah Waters said in 1868 that after a certain depth he could wade out no further,

"not because the water covered me, but because I couldn't reach the bottom with my feet and there I was bobbing about on the waves, head and neck above them, like an empty bottle."

Haven't there been predictions that Salt Lake would eventually completely disappear through evaporation?

A few, but they didn't take into account the declining rate at which salt water evaporates. The more the lake shrinks, the saltier it becomes and the lower the evaporation rate. Salt water evaporates at a rate of only 75 to 80 percent to that of fresh water.

Are there companies that extract salt from the Great Salt Lake?

Several. Actually it's one of Utah's oldest industries. The first company to establish salt mining was the Charley White Salt Works in the spring of 1850. Artificial evaporation ponds are constructed, pumped full of brine and left to evaporate in the sun. At harvest time the salt is plowed up and stored in huge piles. The salt is processed and various grades of salt are produced.

Perhaps the best known is Morton Salt which as of the year 2000 was the largest salt manufacturer in the world. Utah produces about eight percent of the nation's total salt supply.

Salt mining at the Great Salt Lake.

Who owns the Great Salt Lake?

The State of Utah, although it was quite a legal fight to establish. In the 1960s the Bureau of Land Management of the United States Department of the Interior served notice on the Utah State Land Board that it intended to survey a boundary line along the

Great Salt Lake to separate state and federal ownership. A fierce legal battle began that would last for a decade before the final determination was made. The state of Utah is the unquestioned owner of the lake and its minerals, the value of which was estimated in the 1970s to be in excess of $90 Billion.

What's unusual about the sand at the Great Salt Lake?

It consists of brine shrimp feces called oolitic sand. Really! Tiny particles (brine shrimp feces) act as a seed to start crystallization, then aragonite forms around them into pellets or spheres. Lovely thought, isn't it? Oh, to have the sand between one's toes!

Close-up of the oolitic sand from the Great Salt Lake.

Is there a giant whirlpool in the middle of the Great Salt Lake?

Nope. That was just one of the rumors that circulated (no pun intended) for years even after the lake had been completely explored. Another rumor was that there was a powerful tribe of Indians that inhabited the islands of the lake. There wasn't, and the islands are uninhabited.

So, the stories of icebergs in the lake are a rumor too?

Well, actually that has some basis in fact. The extremely salty water doesn't freeze, but the fresh water flowing into the lake "floats" on top of the salt water and *does* freeze. Ice sheets several inches thick can form, break off and float around the lake. One of the largest of these icebergs was formed in 1942. Wind broke up and pushed the ice to a height of 30 feet and length of 100. As ice drifted around the lake people went out and climbed on it. Icebergs were again reported on January 23, 1972 by helicopter pilots from nearby Hill Air Force Base.

What are the "devil winds?"

Violent winds that blow from a southerly direction on the Great Salt Lake. Winds can reach 70 to 80 miles per hour and make it difficult or impossible for sailboats to navigate against them. Once or twice a year these winds can gust as high as 100 miles per hour and cause considerable damage along the south shore of the Great Salt Lake. It is believed the topographical influence of the Oquirrh Mountains causes the winds.

What is a "salt storm?"

Windstorms blow up clouds of salt-dust before a rainstorm and then the salt settles on trees, buildings and power poles. As the salt crystals and water combine they make brine (a salt water solution). Unfortunately brine conducts electricity, and power lines with brine on them begin arcing across the insulators. That arcing results in several dozen pole fires every year. Utah Power and Light Company said that in 1977, 80 pole fires occurred in the month of March alone!

What are the greatest temperature extremes that have occurred in Utah?

The highest official temperature recorded was 117 degrees Fahrenheit on July 5, 1985 at Saint George. The lowest official temperature was February 1, 1985 at the uninhabited Peter's Sink in Logan Canyon at minus 69 degrees Fahrenheit.

Does Utah get much rain?

Only about 13 inches a year. That makes Utah the second driest state in the union after Nevada.

Plants and Animals

Are there any fish that live in the Great Salt Lake?

Nope, just brine shrimp. No other animal can live in the extremely salty waters, except for the Loch NaCl2 monster, and the occasional whale.

Brine Shrimp. Photo used by permission, United States Geological Survey, Salt Lake City, photo taken by Kevin Johnson, all rights reserved.

Wait, what's a Loch NaCl2 monster?

No idea. We just made it up. Don't ask us how to pronounce it either.

What about the whale? Did you make that up too?

No, we did not create the whale, our powers are limited. However, there were once whales in the Great Salt Lake. In 1875 James Wickham was dreaming up ideas to get tourists to Salt Lake City and its resorts. He came up with the brilliant notion of bringing whales to the Great Salt Lake. He brought two 35-foot whales from Australia with the idea of farming and letting them frolic amongst the tourists. (Of course math was apparently not Wickham's strong suit. The whales could grow to a size of 60 feet and the deepest part of the lake is only 34 feet...)

When Wickham released the whales in the lake they swam around for a few minutes, and then quickly swam away. Most people believe they died because of the high salinity of the lake, but for years afterwards there were whale sightings on the lake.

What are brine shrimp?

First the technical description. Brine shrimp, known by their scientific names as *Artemia*, belong to the phylum Arthropoda (joint-legged invertebrates), and class Crustacea (such as shrimp, crab and lobster). *Artemia franciscana* is the species that live in the Great Salt Lake. A female can live as long as 3 months and produce as many as 300 live nauplii (cysts or babies) every 4 days. The nauplii molt approximately 15 times before reaching adult size of approximately 10 millimeters in length.

You may have heard brine shrimp called by their more popular name, Sea Monkeys! Yes that loveable family of amazing fish creatures smiling and frolicking in a world you control, for sale between the X-Ray Specs and the Sterno Grill in the backs of magazines marketed towards the young and gullible.

They're amazing! They're live! They're Sea-Monkeys on Mars!

Of course they aren't monkeys, they don't come from the sea and there's nothing very amazing about creatures so small you need a magnifying glass to see them, but what do you expect for $9.95?

Sea Monkeys were so popular at one time they even had their own television show in the early 1990s. Howie Mandel was the star. He's fought the typecasting ever since.

Today the eggs of brine shrimp are harvested primarily for fish food.

Anything else live in Salt Lake?

Not really in, but around. Two species of brine flies *Ephydra cinerea* and *Ephydra hians* line the shore by the millions. 370 million per mile of shoreline during the summer to be precise. When you walk along the shore the flies form clouds in front of you. Fortunately these species do not feed on man or other animals but are a nuisance because of their sheer numbers. That's 1.37 flies for every man, woman and child in the U.S. for every mile of shoreline. If you'd be so kind to take your share when you leave the Great Salt Lake, it would be most appreciated. Thanks.

Anything besides whales released in the Lake?

Oysters, fish and eels, but none of them survived. One of the eels was picked up long afterward completely pickled. The finder cooked and ate the eel, declaring it "very palatable."

Buffalo on Antelope Island in the Great Salt Lake.

Are there buffalo on islands in the Great Salt Lake?

One of the largest herds in the country is on Antelope Island. The Island is the largest in the Great Salt Lake and is approximately 15.5 miles long by 5.5 miles wide. Inhabited since 1848 it is used for grazing sheep, cattle and horses. Since 1893, bison have been on Antelope Island and as of 2001 the island maintains a stable population of approximately 600.

Are there antelope on Antelope Island?

There are now. The last antelope had disappeared in the 1930s. In 1993 a cooperative effort between the divisions of Wildlife Resources and Utah State Parks and Recreation reintroduced 24 pronghorn antelope. In the 1995 fawning season that population had nearly doubled in size and the herd continues to grow.

Buffalo Point on Antelope Island.

What is the official state animal of Utah?

The Rocky Mountain Elk.

Why is there a monument to seagulls in Temple Square?

There is a monument there because of a plague of grasshoppers that threatened to destroy the crops of the pioneers. In 1854 millions of grasshoppers began devouring the crops and the Mormon settlers had no way to fight them off. Suddenly thousands of seagulls appeared and began eating all the grasshoppers, saving the crop. It was a miracle and in gratitude the Mormons built a monument to honor the seagull.

Today the California Seagull is Utah's State Bird. The seagull monument was the first ever built anywhere in the world solely to honor birds.

Seagull Monument in Temple Square, Salt Lake City.

Beehives are everywhere! Even on bottles of cream soda.

Were there trees in Salt Lake when the Mormon settlers arrived?

According to legend there was only one, a cedar tree. The stump was displayed in a monument on 6th East between 3rd and 4th South downtown Salt Lake City. Unfortunately the stump was vandalized and only the monument remains.

How did the honeybee become the symbol of Utah?

In the Book of Mormon there is a description of a group of people called the Jaredites who flee from the unholy city of Babel. The Jaredites are led by God to a new home in America while carrying "Deseret" with them. Joseph Smith (the first prophet of The Church of Jesus Christ of Latter-day Saints) would translate "Deseret" as "Honeybee."

The beehive represents an isolated, orderly and industrious society, something the first pioneers were seeking in their immigration to Utah. The beehive became a personal symbol for the pioneers and would become the most pervasive symbol throughout Utah. It's a wonder that Marge Simpson never ran for public office in Utah.

Lone Cedar Tree monument.

Does Utah have a state tree?

The Blue Spruce.

What is the state flower?

The Sego Lily.

Does Utah have a state fruit?

The Cherry.

Are cherries what they call "Utah's Best Crop?"

Well no, but the truly perverse may see a correlation (we're not telling). Utah's best crop is babies! Utah's birth rate has always been among the highest in the entire United States. This also makes the population of Utah among the country's youngest.

One thing I've always wondered is what Native Americans used as sunscreen. Any thoughts?

Funny you should ask. The Zuni Indians used the Western Wallflower for sunburn protection. Ground and mixed with water it was then applied to the skin. The plant is found in the northern and central counties of Utah.

Are there other medicinal plants in Utah?

Several, but one that is unique is the Woodland Pinedrops or Pterospora andromedea. This plant lives as a parasite on soil fungi which feed on the roots of forest trees. An infusion of this plant, primarily found in the Uinta Mountains of Utah, is used to prevent nose bleeding.

Any plants to avoid?

Several plants are poisonous but the Foothill Death Camas or Zigadenus paniculatus is perhaps the most well known. It can poison cattle, sheep and even humans who mistake the egg-shaped bulbs for the edible bulbs of common camas. It resembles wild onions but lacks the familiar onion odor. Any part of the plant that is eaten can cause gastrointestinal problems, weakness, loss of motor function and death.

Is it true that Utah has orange dandelions?

Sure does. Found in the mountains above 6,000 feet they grow in the grasses of sub-alpine meadows. The proper name is Orange Agoseris or Agoseris aurantiaca. They look and can be used the same as common dandelions…except they're orange!

Are there any plants in the Great Salt Lake?

Nope, just algae. On the north arm of the lake are reddish pink algae and on the south arm are blue green algae. The color variations are from the differing levels of salinity.

Algae along the shores of the Great Salt Lake.

Famous People

Did P.T. Barnum meet with Brigham Young?

Yes. P.T. Barnum, showman extraordinaire and promoter famous for uttering the line "There's a sucker born every minute" met with Brigham Young in Salt Lake in 1861. Young had become infamous on the East Coast for his leadership of the mysterious Mormons and advocacy of polygamy. Young asked Barnum "What will you give to exhibit me in New York and Eastern cities?" Barnum had to think a minute before replying "I'll give you half the receipts, which I will guarantee shall be $200,000 per year, for I consider you the best show in town."

What did Mark Twain say about Salt Lake City?

"Reports of its death have been slightly exaggerated."

Actually, he said "Salt Lake City was healthy – an extremely healthy city. They declared that there was only one physician in the place and he was arrested every week regularly and held to answer under the vagrant act for having 'no visible means of support'."

Do Mormons have horns on their heads and devil tails?

Yes, but they only show them while inside their temples, which is why they aren't open to the public. All joking aside, people actually used to believe they did!

The early Mormon settlers were a private group and much misunderstood by outsiders. Because their religion was different, rumors began circulating about how different they were, including their appearance. The reality is that Mormons look just like everyone else - no horns, no tails.

Is it true that the Mormon Tabernacle Choir originated when one polygamist's wives asked him repeatedly, in unison, to take out the garbage?

Hmm… interesting theory. We'll check and get back with you.

What record has the Mormon Tabernacle Choir set?

On the 15th of July, 1929 the choir performed its first network radio broadcast of *Music and the Spoken Word*. On the air to this day it is the longest-running network radio program in the world. In 1959 the choir received the Grammy Award for their rendition of "Battle Hymn of the Republic."

Was someone really banished to Fremont Island in the middle of Salt Lake?

That's the story of Jean Baptiste, a gravedigger at the Salt Lake City cemetery. After a funeral and before the grave was closed Baptiste would secretly open the casket one last time. He would strip the corpse of all clothing and adornments. Nobody knew this was happening until a body had to be exhumed for burial elsewhere and was discovered completely naked.

Investigators searched Baptiste's home and found boxes with burial gowns, shoes and other items belonging to the dead. People were so outraged he probably would have been lynched if not for protection by the authorities. For pointers on how to properly rob a grave, be sure to read *True Secrets of Key West Revealed!*

At this point the stories become conflicting. Some say Baptiste's ears were cut off and his forehead branded with the words "Grave Robber." Other reports say the words were written on his forehead with indelible ink. Unfortunately because no records of any trial against Baptiste exist, there is no way of knowing for certain if these things are truth or fiction.

What we do know is that Baptiste was "sentenced" to banishment from humanity, but since he already lived in Salt Lake City they decided to go a step further and took him to Fremont Island in the Great Salt Lake. Henry, Jacob and Dan Miller used the island as a sheep range and had a small cabin stocked with supplies.

Once Baptiste's sentence was handed down the Millers helped local authorities transport him and carry out the sentence. The Millers came back three weeks later to check on Baptiste who was apparently fine and had helped himself to the food.

The Millers visited again three weeks later and the scene was very different. The cabin had been partially disassembled, presumably to make a raft or boat with the wood and it appeared Baptiste had escaped from the island. Nobody is sure what happened to him but nearly 30 years later in 1890 a skull was found in the Jordan River delta; and three years after that a partial skeleton was found with an iron ball chained to one leg.

Many people thought these were the remains of Baptiste but authorities denied that he had ever been shackled in any way. The mystery remains to this day.

What did Spencer W. Kimball do?

He was President of The Church of Jesus Christ who in 1978 had a revelation that allowed black males to hold the priesthood. This opened the doors to membership growth throughout the world.

Were there any black men given the Priesthood in The Church of Jesus Christ *before* 1978?

There was at least one. Elijah Able was born July 25, 1810 in Maryland. He converted to The Church of Jesus Christ and was baptized in September of 1832. On March 3, 1836 Able was ordained as an Elder and given Priesthood in The Church.

What do the Imperial Russian Ballet, Rudolph Valentino and the Utah Museum of Fine Arts have in common?

A young Utah girl named Winifred Kimball Shaughnessy, called "Wink" by her family. Wink became romantically involved with a Russian dancer named Kosloff while she was attending school in Europe. So, she did what any young girl in love does, she changed her name to Natacha Rambova and joined the Imperial Russian Ballet. Hey, we've all had the urge.

The honeymoon wouldn't last long. Kosloff was a jealous lover and pulled a gun and shot Rambova. She survived her wounds but decided to move to Hollywood. That's when Rambova met and married Latin heartthrob Rudolph Valentino. By all accounts the marriage was a happy one that ended tragically when, at the age of thirty one, Valentino died of a burst ulcer.

Rambova continued to pursue many interests including actress, playwright and Egyptologist. She donated a huge collection of her Egyptian artifacts to the Utah Museum of Fine Arts and they are displayed as the Natacha Rambova Collection of Egyptian Antiquities.

What did Dr. T. Henry Moray invent?

Why, the unlimited free energy device of course! Buy yours today! Dr. Moray theorized that there were almost unlimited amounts of energy from the meta frequency oscillations of space.

Dr. Moray was interested in everything electrical from a very early age but his mother wanted him to study business, so he enrolled in a business course at the Latter-day Saints Business College. He managed to study electrical engineering through correspondence and even purchased a share of the Independent Electrical Company. The electrical company collapsed and he lost all his money, but not his dream.

In 1912 Dr. Moray went to Sweden on a mission for The Church of Jesus Christ. There he completed his

LDS Business College.

doctorate in electrical engineering and there discovered the key material to building his "Radiant Energy Device." He left Sweden in 1914 when his mission was finished and continued working on his invention.

Dr. Moray's life would take a turn for the worse in 1921 when he was working on a special project involving interference on telephone lines. He was involved in an accident that seriously impaired his vision. Without any compensation from the company involved, Dr. Moray would search for another line of work. In 1923 he discovered his talent in chicken farming and rare poultry. Finally his financial worries were over and he now had time to devote to finding free energy for the world.

It was about 1929 when he began to demonstrate his device publicly. Unfortunately for Dr. Moray there were lots of people who didn't want to see unlimited free energy. Over the next few years, his life turned into a bad country song. He was shot in his laboratory, shot at in his car (which he had outfitted with bulletproof glass), his laboratory was broken into, his equipment destroyed and his dog was murdered.

Both the Russians and Japanese expressed interest in the device and in 1938 Moray received an offer to go

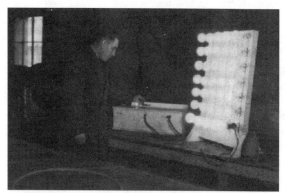

Dr. Moray demonstrating his Radiant Energy device. Photo used by permission, Nu Energy Horizons, www.NuEnergy.org, all rights reserved.

to Japan to demonstrate its weapons potential. (Did we forget to mention he managed to turn the "Radiant Energy Device" into a death ray that when aimed at mice would carbonize them immediately? The mouse appeared frozen but simply fell apart when touched.)

In the end the "Radiant Energy Device" was never patented. Dr. Moray was never able to secure the funding for large scale research and he passed away in May of 1974. After his death his son, John Moray continued his father's work.

Was that the end of Free Energy?

Yes and no. On March 23, 1989, two electrochemists, Dr. B. Stanley Pons and Dr. Martin Fleischmann, from the University of Utah, reported a major breakthrough

in nuclear fusion research at a press conference in Salt Lake City. They claimed to have discovered how to produce nuclear fusion, in a test tube, at room temperature, in a high-school type apparatus. It would be like someone saying they'd just driven to Mars in a 1978 Chevy Caprice Estate Wagon.

What's Cold Fusion?

The theory, in a nutshell, is that the element deuterium, a heavy isotope of hydrogen present in water, can provide a nearly limitless supply of energy by fusing at room temperature in a simple electrolytic cell. An abundant, cheap and pollution-free energy source.

Within two weeks cold fusion was the cover story of *Time*, *Newsweek* and *Business Week*.

The Journal of Electroanalytical Chemistry published the Fleischmann and Pons cold fusion paper four weeks after they received it. It was a classic case of premature publication. The original paper was eight pages long, but was followed a few weeks later by two pages of corrections or errata. That's a quarter of the length of the original paper! Errors included a lack of important experimental detail and even the name of a third author, M. Hawkins. If a graduate student had submitted such a paper he surely would have received a failing grade.

Utah's state legislature moved quickly after the Fleischmann and Pons press conference to establish a $5 million fund to support and promote cold fusion research in Utah and secure patents for the procedure.

The funds were supposed to be released only after cold fusion was scientifically confirmed. A Fusion/Energy Advisory Council was formed and on July 21, 1989 they voted unanimously to accept the Fleischmann-Pons claims of cold fusion. While the Advisory Council was blindly accepting the Fleischmann and Pons claims, the United States Department of Energy found "no convincing evidence that useful sources of energy would result from the Fleischmann-Pons phenomenon." All the money was eventually spent without a single patent or verifiable scientific breakthrough.

What eventually happened to cold fusion?

Deep-freeze. The procedure that supposedly produced cold fusion was flawed; the results were interpreted incorrectly, and the science downright wrong. Cold fusion was a fantasy that eventually faded into the world of the Tooth Fairy and Santa Claus.

Is there really a church named after Jayne Mansfield?

Yes, but it was a radio program. Three men started The Church of Jayne Mansfeild (the last name misspelled for legal reasons) for their radio program on KBBX, a gospel station. The Church was supposedly based on a book about Jayne Mansfield called *Pink Physics* and subtitled *Titty Monster*.

Apparently the author of *Pink Physics*, known only as Princess, received messages or visions from Mansfield on a heart-shaped platter surrounded by orbiting Chihuahuas with messages from her under their collars.

What would happen if The Church of Jane Mansfeild merged with the 24 Hour Church of Elvis in Portland Oregon?

Excellent question. We surmise that the orbiting Chihuahuas would be replaced by pork chops and applesauce.

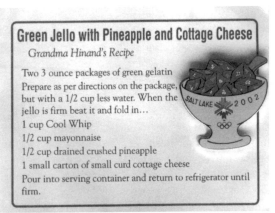

Official Olympic memorabilia. Green Jello with Pineapple and Cottage Cheese pin!

Did Bill Cosby really appear before the Utah State Legislature?

Yes. He was lobbying to have Jell-O® designated the official snack food of Utah, and certainly earning those spokesdollars. The legislators must have liked what they heard because on January 31, 2001 Jell-O® was declared the official snack food of the state of Utah. Maybe they were just excited to see someone famous other than Donnie & Marie Osmond, but the legislators went even further by declaring the week of February 4-10 of 2001 Jell-O® Week. The Salt Lake Olympic Committee designed a pin with a bowl of green Jell-O® and carrots as officially licensed Olympic memorabilia. The pins were hot sellers!

Who was Orrin Porter Rockwell and why was he so feared?

Rockwell was an early convert to and protector of The Church of Jesus Christ, and in the early days members of The Church needed a lot of protection.

Rockwell's legend began on April 6, 1830 when Joseph Smith officially organized the "Church of Christ" at the Peter Whitmer Sr. home in Fayette, N.Y. This would later become the site of Smith's first arrest and persecution for his religious beliefs. Arrests and trumped up charges would continue until January of 1831 when Smith moved The Church to Kirtland, Ohio.

In July of 1831 Smith visited Independence, Missouri and designated Independence as "the land of promise, and the place for the city of Zion." For the next several years The Church would operate between Missouri and Ohio. Unfortunately relations between Church of Jesus Christ members and non-members would slowly deteriorate until 1838.

On July 6, 1838 Smith was forced to move his followers out of Ohio and consolidate everyone in Missouri. But things were about to get much worse.

Amidst this persecution and turmoil Orrin Rockwell joined a secret society formed to protect Church members. The society was commanded by Jared Carter and adherants originally called themselves "The Brother of Gideon." The name came about because it was known that Carter had a brother named Gideon.

Additional names were used including "Daughter of Zion" from the Book of Mormon scripture Micah 4:13: "Arise and thresh, O daughter of Zion; for I will make thine horn iron, and I will make thy hoofs brass: and thou shalt beat in pieces many people; and I will consecrate their gain unto the Lord, and their substance unto the Lord of the whole earth." This would be discarded because the incongruity of bearded rough men and the image of "Daughter of Zion." Other names

Bibliography

Books

Anderson, Bernice Gibbs *The Pacific Railway and the golden Spike 1869 - 1969*. Golden Spike Association of Box Elder County: Box Elder County, UT. 1968.

Angus, Mark *Salt Lake City Under Foot – Self-Guided Tours of Historic Neighborhoods*. Signature Books, Inc.: Salt Lake City, UT. 1996.

Beehive House, The. The Church of Jesus Christ of Latter-day Saints: Salt Lake City, UT. 1978.

Cannon, Hal *The Grand Beehive*. University of Utah Press: Salt Lake City, UT. 1980.

Carter, Kate B. *The Story Of The Negro Pioneer*. Daughters of Utah Pioneers: Salt Lake City, UT. 1965.

Christensen, Vera and Nuhn, Elizabeth *The Big Cache – Fantasy, Fact, Folklore, Bicentennial Edition 1976*. Herald Printing Company: Logan, UT. 1976.

Cuch, Forrest S. *A History of Utah's American Indians*. Utah State Division of Indian Affairs / Utah State Division of History: Salt Lake City, UT. 2000.

Czerny, Peter G. *The great Great Salt Lake*. Brigham Young University Press: Provo, UT. 1976.

Deseret News Staff *Deseret News 1981 Church Almanac – The Church of Jesus Christ of Latter-Day Saints*. Deseret News: Salt Lake City, UT. 1980.

Deseret News Staff *Deseret News 1995-96 Church Almanac – The Church of Jesus Christ of Latter-Day Saints*. Deseret News: Salt Lake City, UT. 1994.

Du Toit, Herman *Vision in the Desert*. Agreka Books: Salt Lake City, UT. 2000.

Gadd, John D.C.; Bliss, Sheldon and Querry, John M. *What's in Utah – Facts, Places and History*. JSJ Enterprises: Salt Lake City, UT. 1978.

Gwynn, J. Wallace Ph.D. *Great Salt Lake a Scientific, Historical and Economic Overview*. Utah Geological and Mineral Survey – a division of the Utah Department of Natural Resources: Salt Lake City, UT. 1980.

Harris, Trent *Mondo Utah – A collection of extreme weirdness from the land of Zion*. Dream Garden Press: Salt Lake City, UT. 1996.

Hill, William E. *The Mormon Trail – Yesterday and Today*. Utah State University Press: Logan, UT. 1996.

Holt, Clayton J. *History of Antelope Island (1840 – 1995)*. Syracuse Historical Commission: Syracuse, UT. 1994.

Huizenga, John R. *Cold fusion – The scientific fiasco of the century*. Oxford University Press: New York, NY. 1992, 1993.

Hunter, Milton R. *The Utah Story*. Milton R. Hunter: Salt Lake City, UT. 1960.

Kennecott's Bingham Canyon Mine – The World's First Open-Pit Copper Mine. Kennecott Utah Copper Corporation: Magna, UT. 2001.

Layton, Stanford J. *Utah's Lawless Fringe – Stories of True Crime*. Signature Books Publishing, LLC: Salt Lake City, UT. 2001.

McCormick, John S. *Salt Lake City – The Gathering Place*. Windsor Publications: Woodland Hills, CA. 1980.

McCormick, Nancy D. and McCormick, John S. *Saltair*. John s. McCormick and University of Utah Press: Salt Lake City, UT. 1993.

Miller, David E. *Great Salt Lake – Past and Present*. Publishers Press: Salt Lake City, UT. 1997.

Moray, John E. *The Sea of Energy 5th Ed.*. Cosray Research Institute, Inc.: Salt Lake City, UT. 1978.

Morgan, Dale L. *The Great Salt Lake*. University of New Mexico Press: Albuquerque, NM. 1973.

Nielsen, Vaughn S. *Golden Spike Tour Guide*. National Park Service, United States Department of the Interior, Southwest Parks and Monuments Association: Globe, AZ. 1975.

Peter, Dr. Laurence J. *Peter's Quotations – Ideas for our Time*. Bantam Books: New York City, NY. 1987.

Peterson, Charles S. *Utah A Bicentennial History*. W. W. Norton & Company, Inc.: New York, NY. 1977.

Powell, Allan Kent *Utah History Encyclopedia*. University of Utah Press: Salt Lake City, UT. 1994.

Roylance, Ward J. *Utah A Guide To The State – Revised and Enlarged Edition*. UTAH: A GUIDE TO THE STATE Foundation: Salt Lake City, UT. 1982.

Schindler, Harold *Orrin Porter Rockwell – Man of God / Son of Thunder*. University of Utah Press: Salt Lake City, UT. 1993.

Shaw, Richard J. *Utah Wildflowers – A Field Guide to Northern and Central Mountains and Valleys*. Utah State University Press: Logan, UT. 1995.

Sillitoe, Linda *A History of Salt Lake County*. Utah State Historical Society: Salt Lake City, UT. 1996.

South, Will *Andy Warhol Slept Here? – Famous and Infamous Visitors to Utah*. Signature Books: Salt Lake City, UT. 1998.

Thomas, Charles D. *Historic Temple Square – The Church of Jesus Christ of Latter-day Saints*. Great Mountain West Supply: Salt Lake City, UT. 1990.

Thompson, Lisa *Gilgal Garden – walking tour guide, an historic sculpture garden created by Thomas B. Child, Jr*. Friends of Gilgal Garden: Salt Lake City, UT.

Thompson, Lisa *Historic South Temple Street Walking Tour Guide*. Utah Heritage Foundation: Salt Lake City, UT. 2001.

Utley, Robert M., Ketterson, Jr., Francis A. *Golden Spike*. U.S. Department of the Interior, National Park Service, Historical Handbook Series No. 40: Washington, D.C. 1969.

Wadsworth, Nelson B. *Set in Stone Fixed in Glass – The Mormons, the West, and Their Photographers*. Signature Books: Salt Lake City, UT. 1996.

Wharton, Tom and Gayen *It Happened In Utah*. Falcon Publishing, Inc.: Helena, MT. 1998.

Wharton, Tom and Gayen *Utah*. Fodor's Travel Publications: Oakland, CA. 2001.

Wixom, Hartt *Utah*. Graphic Arts Center Publishing Co.: Portland, OR. 1973.

Young, S. Dilworth *The Beehive House*. Corporation of the President of The Church of Jesus Christ of Latter-Day Saints.

Zotti, Ed *Know it all! – The Fun Stuff You Never Learned in School*. Ballantine Books: New York City, NY. 1993.

Magazines - Newspapers

National Geographic Vol. 189, No. 1 *Utah – Land of Promise – Kingdom of Stone* BY Donovan Webster, January 1996.

Rocky Mountain Magazine *The Saints Among Us* BY Michael Parrish, January/February 1980.

Salt Lake Magazine's Winter of Excellence 2002 *Legends and Lore* BY Jason Matthew Smith, 2001.

Salt Lake Magazine's Winter of Excellence 2002 *Tall Tales Made Short*, 2001.

Temples of The Church of Jesus Christ of Latter-Day Saints *Concerning the Temple* BY Elder ElRay L. Christiansen, Copyright Corporation of the President of The Church of Jesus Christ of Latter-Day Saints, 1976.

Temples of The Church of Jesus Christ of Latter-Day Saints *A History of Temples* BY Elder James E. Talmage, Copyright Corporation of the President of The Church of Jesus Christ of Latter-Day Saints, 1976.

Temples of The Church of Jesus Christ of Latter-Day Saints *Temples and Eternal Marriage* BY President Spencer W. Kimball, Copyright Corporation of the President of The Church of Jesus Christ of Latter-Day Saints, 1976.

Temples of The Church of Jesus Christ of Latter-Day Saints *Why We Build Temples* BY Elder Mark E. Petersen, Copyright Corporation of the President of The Church of Jesus Christ of Latter-Day Saints, 1976.

The Salt Lake Tribune *The Deseret Alphabet Died With Brigham Young* BY Vania Grandi, December 2, 2000.

Utah State Capitol Building BY Utah Travel Council and Salt Lake Convention & Visitors Bureau, 2001.

Internet Resources

50 States.com – States and Capitals [Weber Publications] http://www.50states.com/ last accessed 11/21/2000.

Angel On Temple is Symbol Of Worldwide Faith [The Church of Jesus Christ of Latter-day Saints] http://www.lds.org/media/newsrelease/extra/display/0,6025,527-1-130-2,FF.html last accessed 9/25/2001.

Brine Shrimp and Ecology of Great Salt Lake [United States Geological Survey] http://ut.water.usgs.gov/shrimp/ last accessed 9/24/2001.

Broadcast Filler: Mormon Tabernacle Choir [The Church of Jesus Christ of Latter-day Saints] http://www.lds.org/media2/fillertext/0,6959,509-1-16,ff.html last accessed 9/23/2001.

Earthshots – Great Salt Lake, Utah [United States Geological Survey] BY Robb Campbell http://geochange.er.usgs.gov/sw/changes/anthropogenic/gsl/ last accessed 9/30/2001.

Oolitic Sand on Stansbury Island, - Tooele County [Utah Geological Survey] http://www.ugs.state.ut.us/utahgeo/rockmineral/collecting/oolitic.htm last accessed 10/4/2001.

Preserving the World's Genealogical Records, Deep in a Granite Mountain [The Church of Jesus Christ of Latter-day Saints] http://www.lds.org/media/newsrelease/extra/display/0,6025,527-1-163-2,FF.html last accessed 9/23/2001.

Salt Lake City & County Building [Salt Lake City and County Governments] http://www.ci.slc.ut.us/info/ccbuilding/ccbuilding.htm last accessed 10/6/2001.

State Parks & Recreation – Antelope Island State Park [State of Utah Parks & Recreation] http://parks.state.ut.us/parks/www1/ante.htm last accessed 9/24/2001.

Summum – The Millennium of Reconciliation – Modern Mummification [Summum] http://www.summum.org/pyramid/ last accessed 10/4/2001.

Summum – The Millennium of Reconciliation – Summum Pyramid [Summum] http://www.summum.org/mummification/modern.shtml last accessed 10/4/2001.

Summum – The Millennium of Reconciliation – The Summum Sanctuary [Summum] http://www.summum.org/pyramid/sanctuary.shtml last accessed 10/4/2001.

Utah Code Section 32A-5-107. Operational restrictions. [Utah Department of Alcoholic Beverage Control] http://www.le.state.ut.us/~code/TITLE32A/htm/32a05008.htm last accessed 9/21/2001.

Acknowledgements

A special thank you to the following people for their time, insight and contributions. Without their help this book would not have been possible.

Allen Woods
Carol and Stuart Varner
Joe Gardner of the U.S. Geological Survey
Ken Sanders of Ken Sanders Rare Books
The Staff of the Utah State Historical Society

Index

N

O

P

Z